U0103009

台灣人物奮鬥系列 2

Fate and Luck

命運・運命
一個鄉下孩子
的台北夢

陳道明 著

博客思出版社

看重自己、勇於追求夢想

we should have confident in ourselves and be brave to fulfill our dreams.

序 Preface

嘉義縣立義竹國中 曾崇賢校長

Chung-Hsien Tseng

President of Yi-Jhu Junior High School in Chia-yi County

　　在一個偶然的機會裡，經桂櫻主任的介紹，認識了陳董事長，當時他已與學區內義竹國小的師生合力出版了一本《陳伯伯的童年記趣》。他主筆書本內文，而小朋友們則依陳董事長的文章，畫上相關聯的插圖。第一次與陳董事長見面相談甚歡，他是一位六十多歲的長者，是義竹埤前村的在地人，國小畢業後就到台北打拚且事業有成。陳董事長的言行談吐溫文謙虛，人生體驗深刻，對人對事充滿感恩，目前手上正有幾本專書出版中。不知其生長背景的人，完全無法想像陳董事長僅有國小畢業的學歷。

Introduced by Ms. Wong, I occasionally had the chance to meet Mr. Chen. I had a great time with Mr. Chen. He is a sixty-year-old elder living in the local village of the countryside Yi-Jhu. He left for Taipei after graduated from elementary school and had a great achievement. Mr. Chen is a humble man who speaks wise words since he deeply experienced life and is very thankful. Other than this book, he had another book with the teachers and students in Yi-Jhu Elementary School. He did all the writing, and students draw pictures according to the contents. Moreover, *The Light of Life* is his masterpiece talking about

看重自己、勇於追求夢想

we should have confident in ourselves and be brave to fulfill our dreams.

III

his life experiences and Buddhism. People who did not know his personal background could never imagine that he only got a diploma in elementary school.

　　與他一面之雅後，陳董事長隨即贈送我們全校學生每人一本他的大作《命運‧運命》，而我也因此有此機緣拜讀。義竹國中目前正全力推展閱讀寫作活動，藉此機會，讓學生寫下對此書的心得感想，除了能深切感受陳董事長的艱辛成長歷程外，更能提醒他們感恩惜福，激勵奮發向上、確定人生目標。而陳董事長更出資將學生們的心得寫作彙整成冊，排版印刷後分送給每位學生。對學生而言，看到他們的作品能留存書籍中，這是多麼值得回憶的一件事。而陳董事長，他選擇用鼓勵學生閱讀寫作的方式來行善，也為其回饋地方的方式作了最佳的註解。身為義竹國中的校長，除了感謝陳董事長對教育的用心與奉獻外，能與自己學生的作品永存書籍中，是多麼榮幸及有意義的事。

　　Having met only once, Mr. Chen gave a book *Fate and Luck* to every student in my school. We are now actively holding activity for extended reading and writing. Through the activity, students could write down their thoughts or ideas about this book. It not only makes them experience the Mr. Chen had been through, but also reminds them to be thankful and cherish what they have got, and to encourage them to be sure of their life goals. Mr. Chen even collected reflections and afterthoughts from students, and fund to edit it into a book. Then he printed out for each student. To them, seeing their own works kept in a book is worth remembering. It worth the most in giving feedback to his hometown, that Mr. Chen is kind to others through encouraging students to read and write.

　　當了校長後，竟已好久不得享受閱讀的樂趣。拿到陳董事長的—《命運‧運命》，我竟一口氣把它讀完，後來又看了第二遍。這是一本淺顯易懂、文筆流暢的書籍，書中描述著陳董事長從小一直到創業有成，奮鬥打拚的歷程。隨著書中的描述，腦海裡想像著其中述及的場景，雖然我與陳董事長的成長背景不盡相同，不過書中提及小時候的玩具，我也有相同的經驗，不禁莞爾一笑。此外，文中雖然沒有艱深難懂的辭句，不過字裡行間，始終流露著陳董事長對己、對人、對事的人生哲學及處事智慧—謙卑、勇敢、樂觀、節儉與樂於奉獻。

It has been so long since I last read after being the president. I read Mr. Chen's *Fate and Luck* at once after I got the book, then I read it again afterwards. This is an easy understanding book with a smooth writing. The book described Mr. Chen from growing up in countryside, to the process of starting his business and his achievements. I imagine the scenes as I read through the book. Though my growing background was quite different from Mr. Chen's, we had similar experiences and I had the same toy. This made me smile. Even if there is no big word which is hard to understand, Mr. Chen's philosophy of life and his wisdom (being humble, brave, optimistic, and willing to give) were truly expressed between words.

最近，正風靡著一位年輕偶像—旅美籃球明星林書豪。由於他在美國NBA職籃的傑出表現及面對媒體嘲諷時所展現出的雍容器度，除了讓他登上美國時代雜誌的封面人物外，美國富比士(Forbes)雜誌更為他發表了一篇文章—「林書豪教我們的十件事」。現在，拜讀陳董事長的大作，再對照球星林書豪所教導我們的十件事，雖然他們生長在不同的世代，成長背景及生活環境全然不同，但此兩位事業有成的人物，他們所展現出來的處事風範及人生的態度，卻是如此類似。他們堅信自己的能力，全力以赴，進而提升整個團隊能力，謙遜有禮，功成不居。

Recently, there is a "Linsanity" trend among basketball stars. Due to his prominent achievements in NBA and the high EQ he has shown when the media mocked over him, he has

看重自己、勇於追求夢想

we should have confident in ourselves and be brave to fulfill our dreams.

V

become the cover of Time magazine. Plus, Forbes had a column on Lin titled *Ten Things that Lin Has Taught Us*. Now comparing Mr. Chen's work to the ten things that Lin has taught us, even if their generation, background, and livings were all different, the two successful people has shown and share the same attitude toward life. They trusted their powers and do their best to improve the group, and still being humble and kind.

　　我們希望義中的學生讀完陳董事長的《命運・運命》一書後，不只寫下心得感想，更能深刻地反省思索，珍惜現今所擁有的優良學習環境及資源，學習陳董事長做人做事的態度，進而奉獻回饋社會。十二年國民基本教育政策推動在即，我們努力在學校中營造一個讓學生能適性發展、多元學習的成長環境，而陳董事長的成功經驗也將成為學子的學習典範。在生涯發展的過程，我們想告訴孩子的是：看重自己、勇於追求夢想，只要肯努力，行行出狀元。

　　We are hoping students in Yi-Jhu Junior High School could not only write their afterthoughts, but also reflected themselves after reading *Fate and Luck*. We hope to see students cherishing the best learning environment and resources they have today, and learn how Mr. Chen have his attitudes toward life then give feedback to the society. We are now in action of 12-year compulsory education policy to create a well-developed and multi-learning environment for students. The successful achievement of Mr. Chen has indeed set a great role model for students. In the process of developing future career, we like to tell our children through this book that we should have confident in ourselves and be brave to fulfill our dreams. There's nothing impossible as long as we paid efforts.

感恩惜福，長者風範

To be thankful and cherishing as being a role model

嘉義縣立義竹國小校長

林曜輝

Yao-Hui Lin

President, Yi-Jhu Elementary School in Chia-yi County

　　欣聞陳董事長要將 《命運・運命》(一個鄉下孩子的台北夢)翻譯成英文，發行中英文對照本，真是替他高興，因為可以將他奮鬥的故事傳頌到世界各個角落，激起人們向善、向上的信念！

　　I was happy to learn that Mr. Chen is having his book *Fate and Luck* translated into English and publish it in both Chinese and English. Thus his story of hard working could spread to the world and encourage people.

　　初次跟陳董事長見面，是在他回故鄉回饋–重陽節招待故鄉老人聚餐活動後，到他家拜訪，因為我剛接任義竹國小校長，一方面感謝他的仁行義舉，一方面替義竹國小的師生感謝陳董事長這些年來對母校學子的獎助。購買器具，發展民俗藝陣—跳鼓陣，讓他成為埤前國小的特色，也讓偏鄉的學生有表現的機會，造就成功的經驗。另一方面又贊助本校樂旗隊購買新樂器，老舊樂器更新後，獲得南區音樂比賽行進管樂70人以下國小組特優第一名的佳績。加上又捐助獎學金，獎勵優秀學生，捐資興學不遺餘力。所以陳董事長回校時，小朋友會以歡欣的心情向陳董事長問好：「陳爺爺您回來了！我們歡迎您！」

The first time I met Mr. Chen was in his hometown. He went back for family gathering banquet and I paid a visit at his house. I was just employed as the president of Yi-Jhu elementary School. I went to thank Mr. Chen for what he has done for teachers and students in my school for years. He had bought equipments for our school to develop the traditional dance as a representative of the school. Also, the dance has promoted a chance for students in the countryside to show themselves. On the other hand, he sponsored the new instruments for the marching band. After the renewing of instruments, they had won the first prize to the elementary group of the marching music competition. He had spared no pains of effort on sponsoring scholarships and rewarding excellent students. Therefore, students would happily welcome Mr. Chen when seeing him on campus.

「命運 運命」(一個鄉下孩子的台北夢)這本書分成三大部分，第一部分是「台北─夢想」，主要是在年僅14歲的時候就要離鄉背井到台北奮鬥的故事。從飯店的清潔工開始做起，靠著自己奮力不懈、努力進取的精神，利用下班時間到補校進修，充實自己，終於晉身到飯店服務專員的階層，真可謂：「英雄不怕出身低，只怕看輕了自己。」第二部分是「當兵 成家 考驗」因為人際關係良好，當完兵後就靠著昔日老同事的介紹，而得到好的工作。這些人脈都是平時一點一滴所累積而來的。生了大病，台大醫師束手無策時，也是因為平時人緣好，好心人介紹好的中醫師幫忙治病才得以好轉。就因為要休養生息，才得以進入中古屋市場，而賺得了人生的第一桶金。有失有得，有捨才會得。「勤為無價之寶，慎為護身之術」在中古屋買賣不景氣之際，轉戰遙控器市場，靠著一步一腳印凡事按部就班的精神去創業，終於打造出遙控器王國。第三部分是「取諸社會，用諸社會」，因為經歷了三次瀕死經驗，生命轉折而感到要感恩回饋社會，除了照顧生命共同體(一起奮鬥的好夥伴)外，更捐資興學、認養孩童，潛心修佛，助人為樂。

Fate and Luck has three sections. The first one is Taipei/ Dream. It was about a 14-year-old fighting for his future alone in Taipei. Starting from a cleaning job, he worked hard and enriched himself to get to the service level of the hotel. Great oaks from little acorns grow, unless you look down on yourself. The second section is Serving in the army, forming a family, and standing the test of time. Getting along well with people, he got a great job introduced by his old colleague after finished serving the army. The good relationship with friends was not suddenly gained. While Mr. Chen was ill and the doctor had nothing to do, due to his good relationship with people, he was introduced to a Chinese doctor who cured his illness. Since he has to rest for getting better, he got the chance to sell the houses in the real estate market for his first million. Sometimes lose is a way to gain. "Hard work is a priceless treasure, and being careful is how you protect yourself". When there was a depression in the real estate market, he transferred to the remote control market. By trying harder and harder, working hard step by step; Mr. Chen finally has his own remote control market. The third section is "from the society, to the society". Since he had faced death three times, he understood the importance to give feedbacks. Besides taking care of our partners, we should sponsor education, adopt children, learn Buddhism, and be happy to help others.

「因為感恩，所以行善」這句話讓人覺得窩心，雖然命運是天定的，但是運命是事在人為，盡自己最大的努力去奮鬥，突破環境的限制，終能扭轉運勢，使自己達到成功的彼岸。陳董事長的故事，就是最佳的證明。

"Because of being thankful, we helped others." This line made people warm. Even though fate is handled by God, we could change our luck. Do our best and tried hard to break through the limit of the surroundings. We could eventually change our luck and cross to the side of our own success. The story of Mr. Chen was the best proof.

明道著書述生平
道理清晰懂人情
成長過程全記錄
功成感恩樂不停

Ming-Dao wrote himself an autobiography
Principles of life made easy
Record all life stories
Success and happiness are appreciated

敲擊生命的亮點
Knocking on the bright light of life

嘉義縣立義竹國中　翁桂櫻主任

Kuei-Ying Wong

Head director of Yi-Jhu Junior High School in Chia-yi County

　　讀完《命運・運命》一書，很難不豎起大拇指：陳明道董事長，真了不起。了不起，不在於他的成功事業，也不在於創立遙控器王國。了不起，在於奮發向上的精神、知福惜福造福的態度以及知恩感恩報恩的作為。

It's hard not to praise highly after finishing *Fate and Luck*. Mr. Chen really did an amazing work. The most amazing thing was not his achievement or his remote control kingdom, but his never giving up and being thankful.

　　義竹，哺育博士的搖籃。但從農業社會進入工商社會，讓就業機會偏低的義竹，哺育了博士，卻留不住博士。如今，放眼義竹，多為黃髮垂髫。以義竹國中而言，來自隔代教養、單親家庭或寄親家庭的比例偏高，孩子茫茫於未來、缺乏向上動力與人生標的。身為教師，我們總苦思著激勵孩子的策略，尋找著孩子人生的典範，努力於透過多元課程與活動，讓孩子找到人生的定錨點、方向與目標。

Yi-Jhu Junior High School is a foundation to doctors. From farming to a industrial business society, Yi-Jhu Junior High School, with low employment rate, has educated many doctors; however could not keep them. Today, Yi-Jhu Junior High School is filled with old and young. Yi-Jhu Junior High School as an example, more families were single parent families or children rose by grandparents that the children lost in the path to the future and have no motivation to their life goals. As a teacher, we were always brainstorming on strategies to encourage children. Also, we tried our best to set role models to the children and lead them to their life goals through multi-cultural courses and activities.

一次偶然的機會，在逸君老師的引薦下，認識了陳董事長，拜讀了他的自傳。勤勞克儉、敦厚質樸的待人處世，一步一腳印、積極進取的做事態度，從談話中，從自傳裡，一覽無遺。不禁驚嘆：典範，就在身邊，何必遠求！這學期，我們的孩子非常幸運，每個孩子受贈一本《命運‧運命》，閱讀了《命運‧運命》，並且在董事長大力支持下，將閱讀心得集結成冊，鉛印成義竹國中閱讀寫作集。

By an occasional chance that I met Mr. Chen introduced by Yi-Jun (teacher) and had read his autobiography. Mr. Chen lived a frugal life and he was always kind to people. He worked hard on everything. I could be so sure from his words and deeds and his biography. I cannot help but gasp in surprise that the perfect role model is right next to me. There is no need to seek. This semester, my children were very lucky to have the book *Fate and Luck* each. With the great support of Mr. Chen, he gathered the afterthoughts and reviews of the book from the students and printed as the reading and writing book of Yi-Jhu Junior High School.

「生命中要有貴人，也要自己有可貴之處。」親愛的孩子，從這本閱讀寫作集裡，我們瞧見無數的感動、敬佩、省思以及自我期許；彷彿也瞥見董事長輕挽各位的雙手，殷殷切切、娓娓訴說著「註冊是保證、商標是責任」的人生觀。那麼，請你一定要持續努力！請你記住這一刻內心的感動，將之轉為行動，創造自我價值，人助助人，助人人助，成為承先啟後的傳人。

"We must be influential to have an influential person of life". My dear children, we could see endless admire and respect, and touching scenes in the book that encouraged us. It was as if Mr. Chen holding hands with the children talking about his concept of life, "registration is a proof; trademark is responsibility". Please! You have to work hard and remember the touch of your heart this very moment to turn the feeling into action. Then be the first one to create your self-value and help others.

最後，感謝國文領域老師的協助與指導，感謝文林老師設計閱讀寫作集的封面，謝謝您們成就這本閱讀寫作集，謝謝您們敲擊孩子生命的亮點。讓我們一起努力，敲擊一個又一個亮點，相信會有那麼一天，繁星點點，譜織成璀璨絢麗的星空。

At last, I would like to thank the help and guide of the Chinese teachers, and Wen-Ling (teacher) for designing the cover of reading and writing book. Thank you all for accomplishing the book and to knock on children's bright light of life. Let us all make efforts and knock on bright lights after bright lights. I believe in the day where the stars shine to form a splendid starry sky.

吉人天相，善者神祐

God Bless the Righteous who walks in His Integrity

台大哲學思考工作坊第八屆社長 余坤興

Kun-Hsing Yu, MD

8th President of Philosophy Thinking Club,

National Taiwan University, Taipei, Taiwan

　　態度決定高度，個性決定命運。一般人常將自己掌握不了的事情歸咎於命運，卻不知一個人的命運與個性往往有極大的關聯。所謂「種瓜得瓜、種豆得豆」、「相由心生、境隨心轉」，表面上無可改變的命運，其實若不是因過去的行為而造成，便是由當下的態度所決定。

　　Attitude is altitude, and disposition shapes destiny. Although it is tempting to ascribe occurrences to fate, there is an undeniable relation between one's fate and one's characteristics. As a saying goes, "as you sow, so shall you reap." Destiny is not as immutable as it seems. In fact, it is largely shaped by our past decisions and influenced by the way we face it.

　　拜讀陳先生過去數十年來的人生閱歷，不禁肅然起敬。作者一生經歷了多少驚濤駭浪，卻總能以平常心化險為夷，事後還不忘感激一路相助的貴人，謙沖自牧的個性躍然紙上。陳先生歷盡滄桑，而後又花了一年的工夫沉澱思維，再以最誠摯的筆觸忠實寫下所有人生體悟，大方傳授給下一代，己立立人的精神也令人欽佩不已。「吉人天相，善者神祐」正是陳先生的最佳寫照。

The more I read about President Chen's life, the more I adore him for his noble character. President Chen experienced the vicissitude of life, sailed through the storms and rough water, and remained humble and thankful to the people around him. After returning from his odysseys, he spent one year to refine his thoughts, and passed on his insights freely to the next generation. His altruism also won him great respect. I believe "God bless the righteous who walks in his integrity" are the best words to summarize his feats.

孟子曰：「人之有德慧術知者，恆存乎疢疾。」安逸的生活固然為人所嚮往，但唯有在困頓中才能砥礪最堅韌的靈魂。期待陳先生的生命故事能夠廣為流傳，讓更多人從中領悟人生的道理。

Mencius once said, "men who are possessed of intelligent virtue and prudence in affairs will generally be found to have been in trials and tribulations." Living in comfort sounds appealing to the vast majority of people, but only after deep sorrow does judiciousness develop. I hope to spread the words of wisdom by President Chen and inspire more people by his precious experiences.

態度決定高度，個性決定命運

Attitude determines altitude, and personality determines fate.

自序
Author's Preface

　　這本書記錄了我一生幾十年來的點點滴滴。我十四歲就離鄉背井，踏入社會打拼，一路走來，嚐盡了酸甜苦辣，至今記憶猶新。利用一年時間，回想自己五十幾年來發生的每一件事，竭盡所能，整理成一本書，完成了我的前半生奮鬥史――《命運‧運命》。這對我來說是一件很艱難的事，可是我用一顆堅定的心去做，克服很多困難，終於完成這本《命運‧運命》。回憶的過程，使我更了解生命的意義，不只僅在為自己創造無限可能，更重要的是能開創更多的利人機會。

　　This book recorded the years of my life. I worked away from my hometown to the big city, Taipei, when I was at the age of fourteen. I experienced lots of things and those memories were still fresh to me. It took me a year to recall every event happened to me in the past fifty years, and I did my best to write them down into a book. To me, writing is not an easy job, but with a strong mind I confronted many difficulties to complete this book *Fate and Luck* eventually. While I was doing memorizing and recollecting things happened to my youth life, it made me understand the true meaning of life. Not about creating infinite possibilities of myself, but most importantly offering more beneficial opportunities to others.

人生說長不長，說短不短。五十年的歲月，轉瞬間就物換星移，人事全非。回想起童年生活的四十年代，與我現今所處的九十年代，五十寒暑的時光，生活、社會卻有天壤之別，其變化之鉅實難想像。

Things changed a lot in these fifty years. The life today is very different from that in the 40's. It will be hard for people to imagine how my childhood was like in fifty years ago.

猶記得當時離家北上，父親騎著腳踏車送我到火車站的情景，直到現在還縈繞在腦海裡。很難想像，我那時還只是個懵懂的小孩子，又沒有一技之長，也沒有任何人際背景，竟然敢離開父母親，獨自踏入社會。這種膽量、氣魄，至今回想起來都不自禁的佩服自己。

I still remember the time when I went up to Taipei city, leaving my family; father rode me to the train station on a bicycle. The scene still runs in my mind now. It was really hard to imagine that I was brave to work away from home and leave my parents when I was an ignorant teenager with no skills, knowledge or any backgrounds. I am proud of myself every time when thinking the past of my bravery and vigorousness.

人生世事難預測，在我的一生當中就曾發生很多預料不到之事。在我剛開始要演出精彩人生時，就差點被病魔打倒。名醫判了我死刑，躺在急診室裡，等待死亡的那一刻，心裡想著自己一定沒有機會活著回家。所幸遇到貴人，最後又能夠恢復健康。這種情況很少人有機會體驗，但卻是我的親身經歷。

Life is unpredictable, and there were many accidents happened in my life. At the time when I was about to perform a splendid life, the sickness came and almost defeated me. Once, a professional doctor announced my death. When I was lying in the emergency room, waiting my death to come; I thought I had no chance of going home. Luckily I met the right person and I got cured at last. I believed not many people have been in situation like this; however, this was my real experience.

想當初我來台北，連寫封信回家報平安也不會。雖然我受過國民小學教育，可是大部份的時間都在田裡幫忙工作，因此畢業時識字並不多，比不上現在七、八歲的小朋友。而如今，做夢也沒想到，竟能親手完成一本書。

I did not even know how to write a letter home when I first came to Taipei. I had gone to the elementary school, but I spent most of the time helping in the fields. Unlike seven and eight year old children today, I did not learn many words while I graduated from elementary school. It is like a dream came true when I finished this book all by myself today.

年紀輕輕的我，就離鄉背井當童工，難免會有思鄉之苦，非親身經歷很難體會箇中的痛苦。然而唯有在困頓中成長，最後才能真正學習到經驗和技能，才能真正創造自己的前程。若說我今天稍有些許成就，就是因為我未曾輕言放棄，堅持到底所使然。

I worked away from home at a very young age. Homesick was an unavoidable problem for a kid. It was hard to understand unless you have been in the same shoes. Learning and growing in the difficulties made me acquire true experiences and special skills that help create my future. The reason why I am successful is because I never quitted easily and always consisted to the last moment.

在事情還沒一一實現之前，從沒想過自己能做得到。所以說：人的命運還是要由自己去創造、掌握、運轉。

I could not imagine what I had today before they accomplished gradually. Therefore, people created their own fate, hold on to it, and control it.

　　我一生的命運坎坷多舛，諸如鮮有人遭遇過的三次瀕臨死亡經驗，最後都有奇蹟出現而化險為夷；此外，經營了三種自己從未想過的事業，結果不但沒讓自己失敗，反而很慶幸自己能有一些成績。雖然不是很大的成就，但我卻很知足現在的生活。這本書的成形，就是當我最艱苦的時候所許下的一個願望—有朝一日，若我能渡過難關，而有所成就時，一定要將自己的經驗整理出來，希望能給予年輕人一些經驗、鼓勵。讓他們瞭解到，真正的成功，是必須腳踏實地，真誠以對的付出。絕非投機取巧、心存僥倖所能達到的。

My life was tough and harsh, I had been on the edge of death three times but luckily the miracles showed up and saved me. Moreover, I managed three kinds of business that I had never thought about in my life. Gladly I have a little success in my career. I may not able to compare with others, but I am very grateful for what I have today. The story of this book could trace back to a wish that I made during the toughest days of my life: if I could overcome all of the difficulties in my life, I will share my success to teenagers to encourage them. Also, I would tell them that the true success is treating others kindly and sincerely. Taking advantages could never lead to success.

　　或許讀者看了本書，可能會心存疑問，懷疑這是真的嗎？

Readers might ask with doubt: are these real?

　　我必須鄭重聲明，我不是小說作家，也非編劇，不會編造故事。本書中所描述的每一件事，均是我個人的一生經歷，絕無造假之虞。正是因為如此，在撰書的過程中，有幾位好朋友，曾建議我花錢請人代寫，可以不必這麼辛苦。但我卻不以為然，這不是花不花錢或辛不辛苦的問題，而是自己的故事由自己來寫，這才最真實、也最貼切。更何況這也反映出自己的個性，一生做事的原則就是親力親為，實事求是。

I must seriously claim that I am not a novelist, nor a dramatist. I will not make up stories. Everything mentioned in this book was my very own experience and there were no fake stories. Because of this reason, I insisted to write it by myself. A few friends of mine suggested me that I paid for some writers to reduce my workloads. However, I ignored their suggestions. This is not about money or workloads, but about trueness. I should write my own story to present my true personality. My principle of life is to do one's best and to pursue the truth.

態度決定高度，個性決定命運。人的一生遭遇到的好事和壞事可以稱之為「命運」，但若把壞事變成好事，則稱為「運命」。命是宿世種的因，運是今生受的果，亦叫做因果。一般人說：命運是前世種的因，今生受的果，是早已注定了，所以命運是不能改變的。但是命真的不能改嗎？我卻不這麼認為。我個人的經驗告訴我，命能夠改變的，就是所謂的「運轉」。如何去運轉呢？種好因就能夠運轉宿世因，改造今世的果，這叫做「運命」。所以說：常做好事，多安慰遭到痛苦的人，誠懇待人，幫助真正需要幫助的人，這些都是種好因，有善因就有善果。好比種果樹一樣，只要用心灌溉，一定能結出甜美的果實。有的人如果遇到困難就怨天尤人，說老天給他不公平的待遇，他的命不好，那他一生都無法得到幸福。其實改好運還是得要靠自己，老天也幫不上忙。人生如果要活得更有意義，就不能被命運主宰，要做一個運命的勇者。

Attitude determines altitude, and personality determines fate. "Fate" is what people face in life, both good and bad. "Luck" is turning bad into good. Fate is the cause you plant for, and luck is the effect of fate. This also called "karma" -the cause and effect. People said that fortune is the "cause" made in previous life. The effect of the present life is destined, so the fortune cannot be changed. Yet couldn't the fate be changed? I don't think so. My personal experience has proofed that fate could change. This is the so-called "fortune changing" or "the change of luck". How do you change your fortune? Planting a good cause could rotate the luck and change the effect of life. This is called "the controlling of fate". Doing good things, being good to others, comforting people around, and help those who really needed help are all ways to plant a good cause. Good causes grow good effects, just like planting a tree. The fruits would definitely be sweet if you watered it diligently. If someone complained every time when facing difficulties, saying that God was unfair having a bad fate, then he/ she could never find happiness. In fact, God cannot give good luck, but you can. People cannot be controlled by their fate to live a meaningful life, but to be a brave warrior who can control and change fate.

寫這本書時必須要能耐著性子，寫出我一生真實的故事，這對我來說非常不容易。我一生中做過好事也做過壞事。我所做的好事，鼓勵自己繼續做好；不好的事，必須隨時提醒自己懺悔。寫完這本書，更瞭解生命的意義，人生需要再努力，不斷的修正自己，精進研讀佛學，並且身體力行，這樣才能完成皈依如來大業。藉著這本書分享我「運命」的經驗和大家結善緣，希望大家在未來的生命中更熱愛自己，心胸更寬闊，最終能無罣無礙、自由自在。

I had to be patient when writing this book. Writing the true story of my life was not easy. I had done good and bad things in my life. The good things I done encouraged me to keep going, and the bad things I done reminded me to regret. I discovered the true meaning of life itself when finishing this book. People have to work harder and keep amending themselves. I shared my "fate-changing" experiences through the book to share with you, hoping that you would love yourselves more in your future life, have an open heart, and eventually would be free and happy.

目錄

台北 · 夢想
Taipei/Dream

生命的轉折
The turning point of life

台北 • 夢想

Taipei / Dream

一封信的機緣

A letter

　　南風吹來心暇逸，在我十四歲那年的某個夏天中午，郵差先生送來了一封信，收信人是父親，但也寫了我的名字，這真是令我喜出望外。我從來沒有寫過信，也從沒有人寄信給我，這封信可說是我生平收到的第一封信，對我而言真可算得上是一件大事。寄件人的署名是一位小時候玩伴的名字，這封信是從大都市「台北」寄來的。拆信的時候，全身緊張到心跳加速。信的內容簡單幾句，大概意思是這樣的：「這裡有一個工作機會，你某日搭乘早上八點的火車來台北，『很急』！到時候我在火車站等你。」

　　In a breezy afternoon of my 14th year, the mailman came with a letter. Father is the receiver, and my name was also on the envelope. This is really surprising. I had never written a letter, and no one has ever sent me one. This letter could be the first letter I got in my life. It means a lot to me. The sender was my playmate in the childhood, and the letter was from the big city "Taipei". While unsealing the envelope, I was shivering-nervous. The letter briefly said, "We are offering a job. Please come to Taipei on the 8 am train. This is an urgent message. I'll wait for you at the station then."

　　生活在農村，對台北的印象，都只能從長輩口中聽到台北是個漂亮又繁華的大城市。台北是台灣生活水準最高的地方，那裡的人每天都有魚、肉可吃，穿著時髦又好看，大街上到處可見到三輪車、機車和汽車。晚上燈火明亮，彷彿是不夜城似的。賺錢機會比鄉下多很多，好像天堂。童年時非常羨慕生活在台北的人，村子裡的人不管在台北做哪一種工作，每逢過年回到家鄉，村裡的人都會對他特別尊敬。農村裡的孩子都很渴望去到繁華城市台北，可是從沒想到自己能有機會去台北見識見識。

Growing up in the farm, my impression about Taipei was from the mouth of adults saying that it was a beautiful fancy big city. Taipei had the highest living quality in Taiwan. People were able to have fish and meat and they wore fancy clothes. Three-wheeled bikes, scooters, and cars were everywhere on the streets. At night, the lights were on like a sleepless town. Taipei offered more opportunities of making money than the countryside; it was like heaven. I admired those who lived in Taipei when I was little. The villagers would welcome whoever came back for holidays from work in Taipei with respect. We farm kids were desired to go to a prosperous city like Taipei, and I never thought that I would have chances to go and experience.

突然接到這個消息我真的不敢相信，這是每個人夢寐以求的機會，只是平常我連想都不敢想。我內心既興奮又惶恐，聽說台北離故鄉很遠，人多又很熱鬧，我從未離家出遠門過，突然要自己獨自一人去那麼遠又陌生的地方，也不確定是不是真的有工作。想到這裡，有點害怕又期待。心裡不斷的在盤算著，我只有十四歲，又沒一技之長，如果去了能做什麼呢？可是如果不去，就會失去這個難得的機會，內心很矛盾。

It was unbelievable receiving the news. This was a chance everyone dreamed for, but I dare not to think about it. I was excited and scared. I heard that Taipei was very far away from my hometown. It had a large population and was crowded. To think of going to a strange and far place alone, never leaving my home once; plus the job offered was an unsure case, I felt scared with expectation. I cannot stop thinking that I was only fourteen, and had no special working skills. What can I do in Taipei? If I choose not to go, then I would probably miss the good chance. I was facing a big dilemma.

　　當時電信不發達，沒有電話可以連絡，無法很快的和我的朋友確認台北工作的情況，只能用猜想的。我告訴我自己，「應該是要謹慎一點，確認後再決定去。」當時我猶豫不決，父母親和哥姊們都鼓勵我去，說：這是一個難得的機會，如果你不去，在農村耕田，不會有好的前途。種田辛苦又吃不好，繁華城市賺錢比較容易、輕鬆，又不必受風吹日曬，吃的也會比家裡好。家人的說法有道理，但是要離家出遠門還是給我很大的壓力。雖然內心掙扎，但是最後還是遵從家人的建議，就這樣決定去台北。

　　At that time, the telecommunications were not so common, so I cannot contact with my friend instantly for further information. Therefore I imagine the situation to myself, and I kept telling myself, "I should be more careful and make sure everything's okay before I go." I cannot make up my mind and decide, but my parents and siblings were all encouraging me to go for a try. They said, "This is a rare opportunity, if you choose to stay on the farm, you wouldn't have a bright future. Farming is really a tough job. Making money is much easy in the prosperous city, and you won't have to work in the rain. Also, you'll eat better." My family was right. However, I felt pressured leaving home. Although it was a struggle in my mind, I still follow my family's suggestion: decided to go to Taipei.

「茫茫大海何處停，貴人指引彼岸行。」
"As mentor guide me a way, I know which way I should go"

踏上夢想之路

On the way to my dream

俗諺有云：「在家千日好、出外世事難」。回想當年，離家出遠門，沒有心理準備，突然要獨自一人，離開父母親去一個很陌生很遠的地方，內心真的是十分害怕。但都已經決定了，如果不去，會對不起很多人，所以我還是鼓起勇氣，到台北去冒險吧！

A proverb goes, "Home is home, be it ever so humble" Remembering the days that I never thought of leaving home and have to work alone in an unfamiliar place far away without my parents, I was truly scared. Since I had decided to go, I would disappoint my parents if I changed my mind. Thus I encouraged myself to set out a journey and have an adventure in Taipei.

一般出遠門都要準備些日常用品，最起碼也要有一個包袱裡面放幾件衣服，可是當時我兩手空空，全身上下只有一件上衣，一件長褲，還有一雙布鞋，手邊沒有其他隨身物品。家人給我的一百元，是我口袋裡僅有的錢。就這樣離開家鄉，要去台北謀生。父親騎著腳踏車載我到火車站，一路上叮嚀著我：在外面要小心、工作要認真、一定要誠實、不可做壞事，到台北要寫封信回來等等。父親的叮嚀和關心，我牢記在心頭，我絕不會在外面做不應該的事，一定要當一個踏實認真的人，不能辜負家人的期望。否則，也沒面子回家鄉了。

People would pack up some daily supplies while travelling, or unless a package with a few clothes. On the contrary, I had nothing but only one shirt, a pair of trousers, and sneakers on. The hundred-dollar bill in my pocket from my parents was the only cash on hand. That is all I brought with me to make a living in Taipei. When father rode me to the station on his bicycle, he kept reminding me to be really careful, work hard, and to be honest not doing bad things. The most important is to write a letter home. I had father's reminder keeping firmly in mind. I would never do bad things or things I should not do. I should be a dependable and earnest man. I cannot fail my family's expectations, or else I would not have the face to come home.

乘坐早上八點平快火車搭到台北，大約傍晚五點就到了。普通車雖然票價便宜一半，但是要到晚上十二點才會到。因此朋友要我乘坐平快火車，以便他下班直接來接我。走進火車站，購買平快火車票花了七十七元，還剩下二十三元，父親要我放進口袋。從來沒出遠門，真的很害怕。進了月台又擔心走錯方向，萬一上錯車搭錯方向就慘了。南下終站是高雄，北上終站是台北，假如搭錯而到了高雄，真不知該怎麼辦？胡思亂想，錯綜複雜的心情，使我坐立難安。第一次出遠門，年紀又這麼小，難免手足無措。

I took the express train at eight in the morning and it arrived around five in the evening. It was only half price for the normal-speed train, but it would take 16 hours. In this case, my friend asked me to take the faster express train so that he can pick me up after work. At the time I walked in the station and spent seventy-seven dollars for the express train ticket, and there was twenty-three dollars left in my pocket. I was really afraid of this first journey. I was even more frightened after I was on the platform, worrying that I might get on the wrong train and went the wrong way. "The last stop of the train heading south is Kaohsiung, and the last stop to the north is Taipei. What should I do if I got up the wrong train and went to Kaohsiung?" I kept thinking and worrying. It was normal to panic about going away from home in such a young age.

火車開了好久一段時間，心才平靜下來。兩個眼睛一直往窗外注視著一片綠油油的稻田，內心寂靜到只能聽到呼吸的聲音，腦筋一片空白。火車運轉發出隆隆的聲音，引起了沉重的氣氛。

在往台北的路途上，我試著勉勵自己說：我一定要認真工作，不要怕苦，要堅強，不可以像故鄉某家的小孩外出工作，因為思鄉沒幾天就回來。又想到家裡困苦，我在外賺的錢給家人，就可以改善生活，這也是我的願望。還有過年回家，一定要買一些農村沒有的東西，來當禮物送給父母親，讓他們驚喜。想到這裡，將來能出人頭地，衣錦還鄉，內心就踏實多了。

The train went on for a long while since I had my heart calmed. My eyes starred at the green fields out the window. I feel so empty and lonely in my heart that the only sound I could hear was my breathing. I had nothing in my mind. The roaring sound of the train made a depressing atmosphere. On the way to Taipei, I tried to encourage myself, "I must work hard, I must not defeated by difficulties, and I must be strong. I cannot be like some other kids in my hometown, running back home from a few days of work because of homesick. Plus, if I earned money for my family, our life could be better. This is also one of my dreams. I want to buy some things we don't have in our hometown back to my parents as gifts at Chinese New Year." Thinking of having a good work and returning home successfully, I feel more dependable inside.

每到一個站，月台上都有叫賣的，有便當、壽司、飲料、餅乾。我從來沒看過這種景象，覺得非常稀奇。雖然我口袋還剩二十三元，可是不敢買任何東西。當天肚子也不很餓，也可能是因為心情太過緊張的關係吧！心想，口袋這些錢也不可以隨便用，以防萬一，一定要到真的非用不可時，才拿出來，所以整天都沒吃東西。火車到了彰化，聽到月台廣播，要去台中的旅客請注意，請先下車，再換到台中的火車。（當時火車分山線、海線）心裡非常緊張，我是去台北的，不知要不要換火車，又不敢問人家。心裡忐忑不安，最後鼓起勇氣問一位阿伯，他解說，「這班火車直達台北終站，你不可以換車。」我心裡這才安定下來，沉悶的心情也很快就消失了。

When arriving at a station, the venders peddled foods on the platform. There were lunch boxes, sushi, drinks and cookies. I had never seen such a scene like that before. Though there was still twenty-three dollars left in my pocket, I dare not to buy anything. Perhaps the nervous feeling inside my heart kept me alerted that I did not feel hungry at all. Moreover, I wanted to keep every penny count, so I did not eat anything for the entire day. The train arrived Changhua. I heard an announcement about transferring trains for the passengers heading Taichung (There were mountain lines and coast lines). I was so nervous at that time. I was heading Taipei but I had no idea about transferring trains. Finally I courageously asked an old man, he explained, "This is a nonstop train to Taipei, so you don't need to transfer." This helped me to calm my heart down and get worries away.

　　我沒有手錶可戴，也不知道幾點了，又不敢問人家，看著太陽快要下山了，心想應該快到台北終站了吧！又開始有點緊張，聽說台北火車站出口分前站、後站，朋友來信也沒說他在哪一個出口等我，我應該怎麼辦？那我下火車是要從前站還是後站出去呢？這該怎麼選擇，令我憂心如焚。又想：萬一朋友沒來接我或找不到我……啊！不敢再想了。但是火車快到站，還是快決定吧！

　　I did not have a watch and I did not have a courage to ask for time. Seeing it was about sunset, I thought the train had almost arrived. I started to panic again. I hear that there were front and rear exits, and my friend did not mention which one to meet. What should I do? Should I go to the front or the rear exit? Not knowing what to do made me panic. Then I thought again what if my friend did not come to pick me… I dare not to think anymore. The train had almost arrived, and I have to make a quick decision.

「離鄉背井孤單行，遠別親人思鄉情。」
"As I leave home alone, the homesickness came along"

到了夢裡的地方
The place in my dream

　　不到幾分鐘，火車果然到站了。我跟著乘客下車，看到人山人海，像螞蟻鑽來鑽去，我愣住了，真的想哭出來，但我還是忍住。從來沒看過這種景象，完全不知該怎麼辦，不知所措。又想著，如果現在父母親在我身邊該有多好！當時感覺好像在做夢一般，獨自一人站在陌生又混亂的人群中，心裡感到非常的恐懼，不敢相信我會碰到這種情況。以前常聽到長輩說：「在家靠父母，出外靠朋友」，現在我真的體會到朋友的重要。愣住了幾分鐘，拖著沉重的腳步，走了幾步又停下來，雙腳幾乎無力再向前移動的感覺，可是也不可以停留在此地呀！最後我往天橋方向走去，站在那裡，看群眾分左右邊出去，一邊人多，一邊人少，心想：反正也不知道往那一邊走才正確，那就向人多的這邊走去吧！

　　The train arrived in few minutes. I followed passengers off the train. It was so crowded. I was stunned and felt like crying by not knowing what to do. I wish my parents were here with me. I stood in the crowd alone and felt like dreaming. The elders often said, "At home one depends on his parents; abroad, will rely on friends". Now I know how important friends are. I stood for a few seconds, then I walked a few steps, then I stopped. My feet could not go any further but I cannot just stand there, so I walked toward an overpass. I stand on the overpass watching the passengers passing by left and right. If I don't know which way to go, I will choose the way with more passengers.

　　就這樣走出去。我只有小孩子的身高，所以路上除了大人的背影，什麼也看不到。當時焦急的心境是無法用言語來形容的。

我心急如焚，只想趕快見到來接我的朋友。完全感受不到周遭擁擠的人群，也聽不到吵雜的聲音，心裡只有祈望再祈望，朋友能很快出現在眼前。

I only had the height of a kid. I could barely see anything but the back of the adult passengers. The panic feeling I had was beyond words, and all I wanted was to meet my friend. I cannot feel the crowd around, and cannot hear the noise. I kept hoping that my friend could be here anytime.

如果現在再給我機會重新選擇來或不來台北，我寧願留在家鄉老實務農，也不要來到這種人生地不熟的地方。雜亂的人群、陌生的環境，忐忑的心始終難以平靜下來。真的很難想像，離開父母獨自一人的下場，會變成如此的惶恐不安。

If I had one more chance, I would rather help on the farm in my hometown than be here in a place like nowhere. I cannot be calm in the new crowded surroundings. I cannot imagine things could be so terrifying when I was alone.

我不停的左顧右盼找尋友人，他不會沒來吧？心想：一定在前面等著我。走了約五分鐘，聽到有人在叫我的名字，原來就是他。看到了！看到了！好興奮喔！眼淚差點掉下，從來沒有這麼高興，複雜的心情無法形容。一見面他就問我吃飯沒？整天沒吃飯，現在才感到肚子很餓。我們就去吃了一碗陽春湯麵（一碗一元五角錢）。吃完後我們走路回去，看到了很「高」又漂亮的大樓（當時最高的房子也只有四層樓），馬路上有璀璨的街燈、很多三輪車、腳踏車，也看到了汽車。原來台北這個繁華城市就是長這樣子啊！

I looked around for my friend afraid that he might not come. After five minutes' walk, I heard someone calling my name. It was him! I saw him! I was so excited that I almost burst into tears. I cannot describe how excited I was. The first thing he asked was whether I was hungry or not. I ate nothing the entire day, but now I started to feel hungry. We went for a soup noodle (it was only one and a half dollar). After dinner, I walked back with my friend. I saw tall and beautiful buildings (the tallest buildings had only four floors at that time). The dazzling streetlights caught my eyes. I saw tricycles, bicycles, and even cars. Finally, this was a prosperous city - Taipei looked like!

「惶恐心情難平靜，燦爛街燈放光明。」
"It's hard to calm while nervous, but street lights were gorgeous and like a sign of prosperous future to me"

社會新鮮人─初出茅廬、膽顫心驚
The fresh graduate—inexperienced and terrified

　　朋友說：介紹你做的是飯店裡的清潔工作，供膳宿，前三個月是試用期，薪水是二百元，等明天老闆見了你一面，應該就可以上班了。隔天老闆見了我的樣子，好像不太滿意。我心知其意，他好像有一點嫌棄我長得黑又瘦。我那時還是個小孩子，來自農村中生活困苦的家庭，所以看起來像是一個流浪兒。老闆從小生活在大城市，又是有錢的人，因此見到這樣的我，當然會懷疑是否有能力。

My friend told me that the work was a cleaning job in a hotel. It offered meals and accommodation but it required three-month probation. The salary is two hundred dollars. After meeting the boss tomorrow, I could start working. The boss didn't seem satisfied with my appearance. I noticed that he thought I was too skinny with dark skin. I was just a kid from a poor farming family, thus I looked homeless to him. The boss grew up rich in a big city; therefore he doubted about my ability.

　　老闆對我說：「你要努力工作，我知道你來自很遠的農村，因此給你這個機會，如果做不好，隨時都會叫你回家吃自己（吃自己就是免職）。」在工作的那段時間，一想到老闆對我說的話，就心有餘悸，不敢鬆懈。回想當時的情景，記憶猶新。其實他是個慈悲的人，否則也不會僱用我做清潔工作，直到現在我對老闆還是心存感念，感謝他願給我一份工作。

The boss said to me, "You must work hard. I know you came from a farm very far away. That is why I give this opportunity to you. Yet if you didn't do well, we'll ask you to leave". At the time I worked there and tried my best on everything every time I think

of those words from my boss. Those memories were still fresh today. In fact my boss is a kind man; otherwise he won't hire me for a cleaning job. I still appreciated him for what he gave me.

（現在想起來我乘坐火車十個小時就到台北，很快又舒適。後來年紀大了，聞到佛法，讀到六祖壇經中惠能大師的事蹟。六祖惠能祖師，從嶺南新州走路到黃梅參拜五祖。我算是很幸福，還有火車坐。六祖惠能走了三十幾天才到黃梅。他在東禪寺還被人看不起，稱他為「獦獠」，是未開化的食人生番之意。當時嶺南新州也就是現在的廣東，是南方山地民族居住的地方。到了黃梅東禪寺，每天盡是做著用斧頭劈柴枝、用腳踏石碓舂米的工作。惠能大師當時人小體輕，還需要在腰上綁石頭增加重量才能舂米。像這樣費氣力，相當辛苦的工作，他都耐著性子一一聽從著去做，不出怨言，不以為苦。六祖惠能是為法而行苦，我則是為金錢而勞苦。）

(I recalled that the ten-hour train to Taipei should be fast and nice. As I grew up, I learned from platform sutra of the Sixth Patriarch in the Buddha dharma. The Sixth Patriarch Hui Neng had walked from Lingnan Xinzhou to Huangmei to visit the Five Ancestors. I was very lucky to ride on the train, but the Sixth Patriarch, Hui Neng, had walked thirty days to get to Huangmei. The people there in east Buddhist temple had looked down upon him and called him 'Ge-liao'. It means the undeveloped human-eating savage. Guangzhou we know today is where Lingnan Xinzhou was. It was where the southern aborigines lived. At the east Buddhist temple, the Sixth Patriarch, Hui Neng worked hard every day to chopped woods and stepped grains. Hui Neng had quite a small figure and he had to tie some stones around his waist for gaining weight to have to strength to step on grains. He endured such hard and exhausting work without complaining. I did hard works for money as to Hui Neng for Buddha dharma.)

吃得苦中苦、方為人上人。離鄉背井到了一個很陌生的地方，從來沒離開過父母，身旁又沒有親人，孤單冷清的感受，使我心裡空虛，更加思念故鄉。每到了黃昏或晚上睡覺，都很想念家鄉的親人，想到他們時眼淚就不自主地流下來，又不敢讓別人知道。心事無人知，思鄉的心情，沒有經驗的人是很難體會的。雖然這種心情很痛苦，可是想要將來有好日子過，無論如何我還是要克服鄉愁。思鄉心情更能激勵我向前走，成功是我奮鬥的目標。

No pains, no gains. To me, it is lonely to leave my family and hometown, working in an unfamiliar place without anyone besides. The loneness made me homesick. When it was in the evening or at night before bed, I missed my family so much that I burst into tears; but I dare not to tell anyone. The homesickness was hard to understand without experiencing it. Although it was such a pain, I have to overcome my homesick. It made me walk forward and toward my goals.

老闆看起來平易近人，但是他要求的工作品質很高。雖然我做的只是清潔工作，但能在台北做事畢竟是我夢寐以求的願望。年紀這麼小，又沒工作經驗，每當工作時總是膽顫心驚。而剛開始只是試用期，老闆隨時都可以要我離職。我常常祈禱這種事情不要發生在我身上，因為這個工作對我來說很重要。當時工作很難找，再加上遠離家鄉又舉目無親，我心裡很害怕被解雇。心想只要肯努力、肯學、全力以赴，認真又細心地把我每天必需做的清潔工作做好，就一定不會讓老闆失望的。

My boss looked nice but he asked for a high working quality. Working in Taipei was my dream though my work is a cleaning job. I was so young without any working experiences, so I worked carefully not to make any mistakes. I was on my trial period and the boss could fire me anytime. I often wished that such situation wouldn't happen to me because this job was really important to me.

A job was difficult to hunt plus my family was miles away; I was so frightened to get fired. My boss will not be disappointed if I paid efforts, willing to learn, and did my best on my work.

「期待賺錢望貴人，感恩之心向前行。」
"I hope the mentor gives me chance for earnings,
and then I go forward with thanksgiving"

飯店的清潔工
A cleaner at a hotel

　　在那裡工作時，前輩教我要如何打蠟、打掃、清洗廁所。雖然我年紀小，可是教一遍就學會。以前很少有櫸木地板，我們飯店的接待大廳就是櫸木地板。櫸木地板要打蠟才會光亮，客人進出又很多，又要隨時保持地板閃閃發光。所以我每隔一個小時，務必要用棕刷拖一次地板，這才能保持光亮。棕刷上面是鐵片，下面是棕絲，約有六公斤重，要用很大的力氣才拖得動它，每次來回要拖十分鐘，地板才會亮。我當時只是小孩子，力氣很小，因此要很費力拖，可想而知有多辛苦。廁所一天巡視好幾遍，擦了再擦，客廳煙灰缸也得保持乾淨，只要有煙蒂就要隨時清理掉。桌、椅、沙發一天也得擦個好幾回。

During the period of working in the hotel, elders taught me how to wax, and clean the toilet. Though I was young, I was a fast learner. At that time, beech floor was rarely seen to use in a hotel lobby hall. The beech floor had to be waxed; plus the guests went in and out through the lobby. Therefore I had to wax the floor anytime to keep it shine. I had to mop the floor with a bristle brush every hour. The brush had metal plates on top and bristle shred below. It weights about six kilos and I had to give all my strength to move the brush. I had to mop back and forth ten minutes to shine the floor. It took a lot of strength for me to do the work. I cleaned the toilet again and again every day. The ashtray had to be clean as well to keep it ash-free. The tables, chairs, and sofas had to be cleaned so many times a day.

　　如果遇到下雨天會更辛苦，因為客人穿的鞋子底部會帶進雨水，所以我要站在大門的旁邊，地上放著一條毛巾，先讓客人擦一擦鞋底再進入。可能我是小孩子，很多客人都非常的配合，運氣好的時候，還會遇到美國大兵給我一分美金（約台幣四角）當作小費，我就會非常的高興。雖然只有一分錢，卻是推動我的心向前衝去賺錢的力量。

It would be a tough work during raining days because guests would bring in raindrop and dirt. I have to stand beside the lobby gate with a towel on the floor to make sure guests had dried their shoes before entering. Perhaps seeing that I was just a kid, the guests were all very cooperative. Luckily, sometimes the American soldiers would tip me with one cent. I was so happy. Though the tip cost only a cent, it was a motivation pushing me forward to work harder.

我的心志很堅定：我一定要做得很好，讓老闆看了會很滿意。過了一段日子，老闆竟然對我有所讚美，這是我最大的精神支柱，猶如吃一粒定心丸，也讓我更賣力工作。即便如此，但是不知何故，每次見到老闆或主管，還是會緊張到心臟蹦蹦跳，呼吸又加速。或許是因為這個工作對我太重要了，我非常怕老闆覺得我不盡他意，而感到忐忑不安。不過，我非常認真又細心地工作，得到了老闆還有同事對我的肯定。

My ambition was firm: I must work hard to impress my boss. A few days passed, my boss complimented on my work. This was my biggest spiritual support. Every time when I saw my boss, my heart beat faster and became nervous. Maybe the work was so important to me and I was afraid that my boss would disapprove my work. However, I worked very hard and had impressed my boss and colleagues.

英雄不怕出身低，只怕看輕了自己。一個有志氣的人，根本不會在意自己的出身低微，只要肯努力，向前衝，仍然會有出人頭地的一天。

Many great men have arisen from humble beginnings. We should not underestimate ourselves. A person with ambition should not mind whether he/ she came from an ignoble family or not. As long as you work hard and keep it going, you will be successful.

「沐雨櫛風艱苦行，克服辛勞學且勤。」
"I worked very hard regardless of weather;
conquer the toil, study hard and diligent"

吾愛吾家
I love my family

　　我要離家時，父親騎著腳踏車載我到火車站，一路上，父親叮嚀的話我還記得：要小心、認真、誠實、不可做壞事，到台北要寫信回來。過了幾天我寫了一封信寄回家報平安，但是又被退回來。我以為是地址寫錯被退，仔細一看，地址雖然都沒錯，可是收件人、寄件人的位置寫反了，而被同仁譏笑。

When I left home, my father took me to the train station on his bicycle. On the way to the station, he kept reminding me: be careful, be honest, work hard, and do not do anything bad; and the most important was to remember to write a letter home. After a few days I wrote a letter home but it had been sent back to me again. I thought I wrote the wrong address but the address was correct. I oppositely wrote the sender and receiver column and my colleagues laughed at me.

　　我當時不會寫信，也從沒寫過信，雖然我受過國民小學教育，可是畢業時識字的程度比不上現在幼稚園大班的小朋友。因為大部份的時間都幫忙田裡的工作，去上學的時間並不是很多，所以不知道應該要右邊寫收信人地址，左邊寫寄信人地址。我把它左右寫顛倒，也因此被寄回來。當時不感到羞愧，心想反正我還小，可以再進修研讀。這又激勵我的進取心。

I did not know how to write a letter at that time. Though I had been to the elementary school, the education level then was not as good as those kindergarteners today. I spent most of the time helping in the fields and seldom went to school, so I did not know the correct column to write the address of the sender and receiver. I was not ashamed of myself and thought I was still young and I had

lots of time to learn. This motivated me to study hard.

　　（寫到這裡，又想起六祖惠能大師，因為不識字，到了黃梅東禪寺求法，所以被人譏笑。他卻不以為杵，默默的修行、悟道。到了最後他以「菩提本無樹，明鏡亦非台，本來無一物，何處惹塵埃」的偈語，贏過當時首座講師神秀大師，而得到五祖弘忍大師的衣缽，這也是他努力上進的成果。）

　　(As I write, I thought of the Sixth Patriarch Hui Neng again. By not knowing any words, he went to the east Huangmei Buddha temple for help. He ignored all the mocking and worked hard on the Buddhism religious practice. Eventually he won the head master of lecturer, Master Shenshiou, with the tagline "Fundamentally no wisdom-tree exists, nor the stand of a mirror bright. Since all is empty from the beginning, where can the dust alight?" This was his achievement.)

　　三個月後，老闆果然給我加薪五十元。自從來到台北，領了三個月薪水共六百元，我只寄回家三百元，剩下都購買我的日用品。從這個月起我每個月可以寄回家二百元，自己留下五十元就夠了。

　　After three months, my boss raised my salary with fifty dollars. Since I came to Taipei, I get six hundred dollars for three-month work. I sent three hundreds home and kept the rest for my daily supplies. After my boss raised my salary, I could send two hundreds home every month and kept the fifty dollars.

　　當時三百元在農村家庭算是一大筆錢，即使有機會做農工，也要做三十幾天才能賺到這些錢。三百元可以給家人買幾十斤白米，有了這些錢，家人就可以吃到白米飯，而不用每餐都吃地瓜飯。我心想，家人收到這筆錢一定很高興，想到這裡，內心感到非常激動：「今天終於也有能力賺錢幫助家人了！」自己差點掉下眼淚，這真是令人興奮！這種感受，如人飲水冷暖自知，是外人無法體會的。

Three hundred dollars was a lot of money for a farming family. Even if one has a chance of being a farm worker, he/ she had to work 30 days to earn three hundred dollars. The money could buy weights of rice for my family. With this money, my family could have rice instead of sweet potatoes every meal. When thinking that my family would definitely be so happy, I feel so excited. I finally had the chance to earn money for my family. I almost touched with tears and excitement. The person who drinks it knows best whether the water is hot or cold. This is the feeling one cannot understand without having the personal experience.

「旭日東昇見光明，回饋家人感溫馨。」
"I could see the future when the rising sun; I feel
warm when the contributing my family"

自我的提升
Improving myself

　　我工作的飯店，主要是接待外國旅客住宿。在這種環境工作的服務專員，必須會講英文和日文，因此他們薪水都很高，有時候客人還會給小費。那時候，我很羨慕服務專員，賺錢多、工作又輕鬆，但一定要會講外語。這讓我很沮喪，我完全不懂外語，連國語都很差勁。可是在這工作期間，經歷了社會的訓練，也懂了一些未來生存的道理，了解一定要找機會去研讀中文和外語，這才有好的將來，只做清潔工作是沒前途的。

The hotel I worked for mainly receives foreign guests. One had to speak both English and Japanese to work there as a service commissioner. In this case, they were well paid and sometimes tipped by the guests. I admired those service commissioners for their high payment and easy job. However, the service commissioner had to have the ability of speaking foreign languages. This frustrated me since I understood none of the foreign languages. I was not even good at my own language. Nevertheless, as I worked there, I practiced and experienced from the society and had understood some principles of life. I had to study my own language and foreign languages when having the opportunity; or else, a cleaner had no prospects.

　　我的工作時間是早上五點半到晚上五點，每個月公休一天，所以自己可用的時間也不多了。經過一段日子，有個機緣，得知青年服務社在舉辦中、英文初學課程，每個月學費五十元，又是夜間補校，我可以下班後再去上課。我立即報名加入。我態度恭敬、謙虛，所以旁人都肯教導我。古人有句話說的是：有心求功名，一定可以得到功名；有心求富貴，一定可以得到富貴。但前提是，一個人要在社會生存，必須誠懇的與人相交，態度上應該是謙虛，待人以禮。

My work time started from five in the morning to five in the afternoon. I got merely one day off every month which means that I did not have much personal time. Days passed, for some reason, I noticed that the teenage service center was opening Chinese and English basic language classes. The tuition was fifty dollars a month and it was also night classes. I could go after work. I signed up for the class right away. I was humble and respectful so the people around were willing to teach me. Those who have their hearts set on attaining success and fame will surely attain success and fame. Those who have their hearts set on attaining wealth and position will surely attain wealth and position. To survive in the society, the premise is to treat others sincerely, and be humble and well mannered.

　　一個驕傲的人，或不懂禮貌的人，誰也不肯去教導他。我了解這個道理，所以我都以謙虛的態度去請教別人，去學習別人的優點，這都是努力進修不可缺少的。我就依照這種方式去做，學校老師和同學都對我很友善。可能我年紀最小，又很認真聽課，因此進步很快。不但學了國、英文，也學到了做人處事的道理，能有今天的成就，我非常感謝他們。

Nobody likes to teach an arrogant and rude person. I understood the principle well, so I asked for advices with a humble and respectful manner. Also, I learned from others' advantages while I improved myself. By doing so, the teachers and students in the school treat me nicely. I paid full attention in class and studied really hard so I improved a lot. I learned not only Chinese and English, but also the principles of treating others. I truly appreciated them for what I had today.

　　雖然同事都鼓勵、讚美又佩服我好學的精神，可是也有一位同仁說：像你現在的程度去研讀中、英文要等到何時才學會？當時我不認為他在譏笑我，其實他的話也是事實，因為沒有基礎，要學好英文一定很難。這句話我銘記在心，也使我更加努力去學習。直到現在，這句話的聲音還一直縈繞在我的心中，就這樣激勵我，給我振作向前衝的動力。

Even though my colleagues encouraged, praised and admired my learning attitude, one of the colleagues said to me that with my language level, when would I be able to learn it? I did not take that as mocking or despising me. In fact, I considered his words as a truth. It was really difficult to learn English without any basic knowledge. I remembered what my colleague said and tried harder to learn. The words are still in my mind. They encouraged and motivated me to move forward.

每個人都是從不懂開始學習，人一出生就是什麼都不會的，皆要靠自己去學。如果實事求是、按部就班、加倍努力就能成功。每個人的學習過程都是一樣的，例如剛出生的嬰兒，開始學喝奶、講話、走路……，一直到成人，什麼事物都得靠自己去做好。所以說，不懂就是要專心學習，這是成功的「不二法門」。今生有一點成就與這位同仁的一句話也很有關係，直到現在我還是很感恩他。

Everyone starts from zero. We know nothing from the beginning and we have to learn. Success is for those who did try their best and do their best. Everyone had the same learning process such as a newborn, they learned to eat, talk, and walk. From a baby to a grownup, everything has to be learned by ourselves. Therefore, we learn when we don't understand. This is the only way to success. What I had today has very much to do with what my colleague said to me. I still appreciated him.

日子過得很快，一轉眼，來台北過了四個夏天。在這四年當中，我一直很認真的在找機會擺脫清潔工作。我做清潔工作的這段時間中，了解到能跟同事建立良好的關係是非常重要的。如果有不懂的事，可以請教他們，有機會他們也會拉我一把。我對同事都很尊敬，因此他們都很疼愛我。

Time flies, it had been four summers since I came to Taipei. During these four years, I tried to get rid of the cleaning job. I understood the importance of establishing a good relationship with colleagues. I could ask for help when I had problem and they would give a hand. I respected all my colleagues and they treated me well.

後來人事變動，他們都向老闆推薦我當實習服務專員。所以非常幸運，在我十八歲的時候，就晉升為試用服務專員。以前的辛苦，現在就嚐到甜美的果實。薪水當然比以前多，所以我每個月寄回家給父母親的錢都足夠他們生活。剩餘的錢，我還是很節省的用。買衣服的時候，總是考慮好久才決定，如果買了，會因為捨不得把錢花掉而失眠。在那個時候就有了一個觀念－－「花錢慢慢來，賺錢快快去。」

There was a big shift among the personnel, and the colleagues recommended me as an intern service commissioner to the boss. Luckily, I was promoted as the trial service commissioner when I was at the age of eighteen. The hard beginning makes the good ending. Undoubtedly my salary raised and the money I sent back for my family enabled them to live happy lives. I saved some money with me but I used it carefully. I always think twice when buying new clothes and I would feel painful every time when spending money. I had a thought in my mind: "spend slowly and earn fast".

「一心堅定求前程，勇於表現萬事成。」
"I pursue my own goal solidly; it could be
succeed that I behave myself well"

當兵、成家、考驗

**Serving in the army, forming a
family, and the testing of life**

蛻變─從男孩到男人

From a boy to a man

　　當了兩年服務員之後，也就二十歲了。當時年滿二十歲就必須服兵役，這和現在相同。聽說當兵非常的辛苦，除了身心有障礙的人，每個男人都一定要去。然而，當兵是男人對國家的義務，想要將來有成就，必需經過當兵嚴格的訓練，服完兵役才算是男子漢，是真正開始踏入社會打拼的第一步。剛入伍前八週是訓練體能和紀律，真的有夠辛苦。

After being a service commissioner for two years, I was twenty years old. We have to serve in the army when we were at the age of twenty. I heard that it was tough in the army. Everyone has to go, except those disabilities. It is the men's duty to serve in the army. One must be strictly trained to have special achievements. A boy would truly turn into a man after serving in the army and that is his first battle to work before entering society. The first eight weeks were the physical and discipline trainings. That was really tough.

　　有一次經驗讓我印象非常深刻永難忘懷：因為棉被沒摺疊好，而被罰全副武裝。午餐後沒休息，就被叫去處罰。當水泥地上最燙的時候，要我蓋著棉被躺在地上，睡了大約半個小時才讓我起來。被罰完了，爬起來整個人全身都濕了，好像剛從水裡出來一樣，可是還要忍著，不但不許有怨恨，還要表現出感恩，這是當時當兵訓練的一種方式。

There was an unforgettable memory: I had been punished due to not folding my blanket right and my naptime after lunch had been cancelled. I was told to sleep with my blanket covered on the burning cement floor during the hottest time of the day. After half an hour, I got up and I was soaking wet with sweat. I had to endure

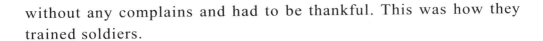

without any complains and had to be thankful. This was how they trained soldiers.

　　我抽到的兵種是特種兵，規定服役三年。但運氣很好，分配到運輸兵，因為國防部命令更改，運輸兵從民國五十八年起，只要服役兩年就可以退伍（剛好從我當兵的那年開始）。

I was a special force soldier and must serve in the army for three years. However, I was lucky to be assigned to be in the transportation corps. The Ministry of National Defense had modified the laws and announced that the transportation corps had to serve merely two years in the army from the 58th year of the Republic Era (that was the year I started to serve in the army).

「軍民同心國家興，皓月當空照光明。」
"When the army-civilian with great royalty to the country which leads to prosperous; when it is a bright moon hung in the sky it has a bright future"

插曲—十塊錢的故事

An episode—a story of ten dollars

　　在當兵的二年中，發生了一件令我印象非常深刻的事，到今天我還是記憶猶新，這不但警惕我，更給我往後在社會立足上很大的幫助。

A very important incident happened during the second year of my army life. That alerted me, and also helped a lot when I started to work in the future.

　　有一天晚上外出散步，遇到一位老奶奶，她揹著一個小孩，右手又牽一個。這位奶奶問我「這條路是到台南茄萣嗎？」我回答是的。奶奶說了一句阿兵哥謝謝，然後牽著小孩轉身就急著再趕路。我突然心想，怎麼不坐車呢？走路大約要二、三個小時。我立刻叫住她：「奶奶，客運就在附近呀！」她回答我：「沒錢買車票，我們要趕路回家，我兩個孫子從中午到現在都還沒吃飯。」我趕緊替奶奶買了一張車票（當時小孩乘坐客運是免費），還買了兩個麵包給小孩子吃，當時奶奶感激到掉下眼淚來。

I bumped into an old lady one night when I was walking on the street. She was carrying a child on her back and holding another child. The old lady asked me whether the road ahead was the road to Chieding, Tainan. I answered yes. The old lady thanked me and turned away with the children in a hurry. Suddenly I realize that it took two to three hours to walk there, so I yield, "Ma'am, the bus station is somewhere nearby." She answered, "We don't have money for the tickets. We have to hurry home. My two poor grandchildren haven't eaten since noon." I bought a ticket for the old lady (the seats on the bus for children were free) and bought

some bread for the children. The old lady was touched to tears.

　　我陪著奶奶等客運到站的那段空檔時間，她說出今天的行程和原因，她們三個人早上三點就從家裡——台南茄萣鄉走路起程到崎山，探望在三個月前送給人家當養女的小孫女。這些日子以來她們非常想念她，心又不捨她送給人家當養女，所以決定去見她一面。

　　I accompanied the old lady as she waited for the bus. She told me their plans: The three of them started to walk at 3 in the morning from Chieding to Chihsan visiting another granddaughter who was adopted by a family. They have missed her these days and been reluctant to give her up, so they have decided to meet her.

　　世事難預料，也許是命中注定。奶奶提起一年前她兒子突然生病往生，而媳婦又離家出走，留下這三個孩子，讓她獨自一人照顧。她年紀大了，又沒固定收入，只能做些臨時工過日子，扶養她們也有困難，因此送一個給人家當養女，可以減輕她的負擔。我聽完這些話，當時也掉下淚來，所以對這件事印象深刻，直到今天還記得。

　　Things happened unexpectedly. The old lady mentioned that her son died from sickness a year ago and her daughter-in-law ran away from home. She took care of the three grandchildren all by herself with an unstable income. She had to do some tough temporary job to raise the grandchildren but it was still too difficult to raise three at a time. Therefore she had to send one granddaughter to another family. I burst into tears after hearing her story. That was an unforgettable story.

　　我只花了十塊錢，就能讓生命更有意義。從那個時候，我了解到幫助真正需要幫助的人，才是真快樂。所以我一直感謝奶奶，因為與她的偶遇，才能給我佈施的機會。這也激勵了我，日後更努力賺錢。主要是覺悟到，當自己年老了若沒錢會很可憐，因此我隨時提醒自己未來要努力賺錢並且存起來，才不會遇到像這位奶奶一樣沒錢的困境。（農村的長輩以前常說要真誠地做人，好人自有好報，真誠的人一生都會得到別人的幫助，所以那時我毫不猶豫幫助那位老奶奶。一個人只要真誠地待人處事，就會得到好報。而今天的我衣食無缺，生活幸福安樂，不正是印證了先人的教誨嗎？）

I spent only ten dollars and a life became more meaningful. From then on, I realized the true meaning of helping those who needed help, and that made me truly happy. I thanked the old lady too. Because of meeting her, I got the chance to give. This encouraged me to work harder. I also realized that it was difficult to live without money when I grow older. Thus I told myself to save money to prevent the tough situation like the old lady. (The elders from the farm always say to be honest because if we treat people nicely, others would treat us nicely too. Therefore I did not hesitate to help the old lady. One would definitely be treated nice if he/she treat others nicely and tried hard on everything. I am financially independent and have lived a happy life today. Isn't this the best proof of what the elders had taught us?)

「誠懇助人積善因，生命意義互關心。」
"When we are sincere to others we can accumulate a
good action lead to good rewards; when we can take care
for each other we know the meanings of life"

揮別單身—成家
Farewell, my single life

從軍中退伍後又是另一段新的人生的開始。六十年代很難找到好的工作，很幸運的是，以前的同事們在其他飯店都當上了主管的職位，他們以前就很照顧我，所以請他們幫忙找份工作，很快就找到了。

It was a new start after I discharged from the military service. Job-hunting was really difficult during the 60s. Luckily, my old colleagues were all directors at other hotels. With their offer, I quickly found a job.

真誠的態度，到最後會得到別人的幫助，像這次就是因為有他們的幫忙，我才能得到一份很好的工作。二十三歲我就結婚，生了一個兒子、一個女兒，組成了一個非常美滿的家庭。雖然當時薪水很不錯，但是我們還是很節儉，不會亂花錢，只想要擁有自己的房子住，不必再跟人家租。因為每個月付房租，最後房子還是別人的。所以當時就有置產的觀念，要擁有真正屬於自己的家。尤其，有了一個家庭，住的地方最為第一要事，因此計劃要買房子。四年後，在台北市當時算是郊區的地方，買了一層公寓樓房。現金七萬元，貸款十二萬，就這樣擁有屬於自己的家。

People would be willing to help if you were honest and kind. I got married at the age of twenty three and had a wonderful family with a son and a daughter. Although I got a good income, we tried our best to save more money in order to afford our own house. I had the idea of buying our own property and wanted to have our own home, because no matter how long you paid for the rented house, it still wasn't yours. Especially when I have a family, the priority would be having a place to live. Four years later, I bought an apartment at Taipei city where it was considered countryside. We had our own house for seventy thousand cash and loaned 120 thousand dollars.

　　建商交新屋，牆壁只有簡易粉刷，舖的是塑膠地板，整棟房子空無一物，我們就這樣先住進去，等到有錢再慢慢添購傢俱。因為是自己的房子，就算沒有什麼設備，住起來也還是非常的開心。在家裡每天心情都很好，非常的快樂，這也許是因為擁有自己的家，讓我有很大的成就感吧！從現在開始，不用再付租金，家鄉的家人也為我高興。自從離開家鄉至今有十二年了，真的想不到今天有能力在大台北買樓房。有了自己的房子，對自己更有信心，也會更加努力去做事。那時覺得，能擁有自己的不動產是一生中最快樂的事，活在世間真美好。

The house was empty with whitewashed walls and plastic floors. We lived in the house and would add in furniture when I had enough money. Since it was our own house, we were still happy though there was nothing inside. It was like accomplishing and fulfilling a hope. My family was happy for me because I would not have to pay the rent anymore. It has been twenty years since I left my hometown. I cannot believe that I could own a house in Taipei. I became more confident and motivated to work harder. Life's wonderful.

「勤儉積德有善報，願望達成自創造。」
"When we have the industrious, thrifty and also
accumulate virtue then we can reward for good deeds;
our wish will be accomplished by one's own"

生死存亡的試煉
The trials of life and death

　　「人無千日好，花無百日紅」、「天有不測風雲、人有旦夕禍福」，這兩句話正是我這一生的寫照。我這一生當中，有過三次瀕臨死亡的經驗，每次都非常驚險的渡過。第一次是十一歲時，游泳溺水。第二次是在二十九歲時，生了很嚴重的病，住進台大醫院急診室，醫生報告診查結果，只有八個字—「無藥可救，準備後事」，這好像是被判了死刑，我年紀這麼輕，又沒犯過什麼嚴重的錯，竟然會遭此橫禍！自己都感到不解。這是一般人都無法承受的。好不容易剛建立一個家庭，又有新房子住，就這樣要我離開人間，老天為什麼這麼殘忍對待我，難道不再給我活下去的機會嗎？真不敢相信，這是事實嗎？還是老天在開我玩笑？

　　Nothing good lasts forever; all good things must come to an end. Accident will happen. These two lines could be the description of my life. I had three experiences of verge on death, and every time I dangerously survived. The first time happened when I was eleven; I almost drown. The second time was when I was twenty nine years old; I got seriously ill and had to live in the emergency room. The doctor wrote four letters on the report, "Hopeless. Prepare a funeral." All of a sudden, he sentenced me to death. I was so young, and I did not do anything wrong or illegal. Why should this happen to me? I had my own family after all and I had my own house, but I can no longer live. Why was the God treating me so cruel? Can't I have a chance to live? I could not believe that this is real. Or was the God fooling me around?

　　我無奈的躺在病床上，一遍又一遍想著，為什麼？為什麼？為什麼這種事會發生在我身上？我身為一個男人，剛開始要為了家庭負擔起責任，就面臨這種事。當時我並不怕死亡，內心卻非常的不安。我知道父母親和妻兒對我的病情一定非常的擔憂，萬一我有個三長兩短，他們往後的日子會如何？我就這樣撒手西歸，會連累很多人的。在面對死亡來臨的時間裡，我的內心其實並未稍有平靜的時刻，終日只是想著家人未來該怎麼辦？身體受著病魔的摧殘，內心則滿佈著罣礙，就天天活在這種內外煎熬中，這種痛苦，沒切身遭遇過的人，是無法體會我當時的難受。

I lied on the hospital bed thinking again and again, why should things like this happen to me? I started to have responsibilities to my own family then I got ill. I was not afraid of death but I felt anxious inside. I knew that my parents and my wife would worry that how were they able to live if I passed away. Their live would be tough if I was gone. During the time I faced death; my heart could not calm and kept worrying about my family and wife. I was physically and mentally ill. One must get the same experience to be able to understand the feelings.

　　一家四口要靠我吃飯，有時候想到小孩這麼可愛，年紀又這麼小，如果沒辦法繼續照顧他們……啊！想到這裡真是令我牽腸掛肚，不敢再想下去。如果沒有結婚，只有一個人也不會感受到這樣的心痛。當時我非常憤恨不平，怨恨老天竟然給我這樣的不平等待遇。

The entire family depended on me. I thought of my lovely children. What if I had no chance to take care of them? Gosh, I could not take this any longer just to worry about them. If I had not got married, I would not feel so painful. I was so frustrated and angry that God treated me so unfairly.

　　十四歲就到台北打拼，剛開始要演出我精彩的人生，就將要被病魔打倒，心想，一定要戰勝，絕不可被打敗，一家四口要靠我生活，父母養育之恩未報。現在我要面臨心靈受的折磨、身體上的痛苦，像這種超級不安的日子，只能憑藉堅毅的意志力來支持度過。不斷的鼓勵自己，我一定要站起來！站起來！

　　I struggled to work for a living in Taipei when I was fourteen years old, the age when my life truly begins. Then I was about to be defeated by the illness. I kept telling myself not to be defeated and I have to stay strong. I had my family and parents to take care of. Now I had to face the pain physically and spiritually. I had to stay strong when going through the anxious life like this. I kept encouraging myself that I must stay strong.

> 「橫禍竟然從天降，牽腸掛肚費思量。」
> "The unexpected calamity was descended from heaven;
> we scratch my head with deeply worried"

生命中的奇蹟
Miracles in my life

　　台大醫院沒空病房，我就在急診室躺了三天三夜。聽說要有特殊關係安排病房比較快，我是農村來的，沒有背景或人脈，到了第三天，還是等不到病房。在急診室的最後一個晚上，我感覺冰冷從一雙腳直延伸到接近心臟，只剩下心臟以上還有知覺。心想生存機率大概很渺茫了，一反常態的，當時我的心中竟然是出奇的平靜。

　　I stayed in the emergency room for three days and nights because National Taiwan University Hospital did not have any empty ward. I heard that having personnel relationship with the hospital staff could help arranging the rooms faster. I came from a farm village without any relationship, so I couldn't get a ward even though I had already lain there for three days. When lying in the emergency room during the last night, I felt the coldness from the tip of my toe to my heart. Only the part above my heart had feelings. I thought I had little chance to live but I felt extremely calm in my heart.

　　就在這個關鍵時刻，奇蹟出現－－前幾天，一位親戚來探病時，提起一位中醫師。他說這位中醫師醫術高明，醫德又好，非常的慈善。可是當時西醫醫院不允許中醫師到醫院看病人，並且病人也不可以在醫院裡喝中藥。父親知道我已經快不行了，醫生又說無藥可救，真的束手無策，於是不顧一切，偷偷的請這位中醫師到台大急診室來。由於中醫師他有虔誠宗教信仰，所以也很慈悲的接受家父的要求，立即到台大急診室來。中醫師幫我把脈約三分鐘後，說：「要急速到中藥行煎藥。」他開出一張處方箋，給父親和大哥。中醫師說：現在是子時了，藥行已關門，你們到中藥行直接敲門告知是我要你們來買中藥，並且還要請他煎好中藥。因為他是我的好朋友，所以一定會幫忙。又說：喝完第一帖藥二個小時之後，如果心臟以下有恢復知覺，就再喝第二帖藥，如果沒改善，可能無救了。

It was a miracle- a relative came for a visit and mentioned a Chinese medical doctor a few days before. He said the doctor was kind with very good skills and morality. However, the hospital did not allow the Chinese medical doctor to work there and the patients could not drink Chinese medicine in the hospital. My father knew that I could not hold any longer and my doctor had nothing to do to help me. Therefore, no matter what it takes, we invited the Chinese medical doctor to the hospital. The Chinese medical doctor had a devout religion, so he kindly accepted my father's request and went to the hospital. He checked my pulse for three minutes and said, "You have to decoct the herbal medicine right away." The doctor gave us a prescription then said again, "it's midnight now and the clinics are going to be closed soon. You could knock on the door and tell them that I sent you there. Asked him to decoct the medicine for you because he is my friend and he would be willing to help. After you drink the first dose for two hours, drink the second one if the body parts beneath your hearts start have feelings. If nothing works, then I have already tried my best"

父親依照中醫師的指示，去中藥行抓了藥，就在中藥行等煎藥。煎好就提著中藥火速奔回台大急診室，把中藥倒進我的嘴巴。喝完中藥二個小時後，心臟以下真的慢慢感到熱又有知覺，當然又喝了第二帖藥。喝完第二帖藥，感覺又好一些，病情更加穩定。不過後來還是等不到病床。心想，反正喝了中藥病情感覺好很多，因此決定離開急診室回家。

My father did what he has told, and grab some medicine from the Chinese medical clinic then waited for the decocting at the clinic. After that, he rushed back to the hospital and fed me the medicine. My body beneath my heart did have feelings after drinking the medicine so I drink the second dose. I felt much better after the second dose and my problem seemed settled. I thought I had recovered much after the medicine so I have decided to go home.

有了這位中醫師的藥方，就這樣離開台大醫院急診室。（沒有這位著名大中醫師，我可能已經往生，想起他的醫德風範，如今記憶猶新。他不但救了我的生命，也影響我的德行，給我往後在社會上做人處事很大的幫助。他的兒子是現任真理大學宗教系的張博士，直到現在我還是非常感恩他們一家人。）

Due to the help of the Chinese medical doctor, I left the hospital. (Without the help of the doctor, I might not live. I still feel fresh when remembering his attitude. He not only saved my life, but influenced my morality. He really set a good role model for me. His son, Dr Chang, is the chair of the religion department in Aletheia University. I still appreciated their family.)

「生存渺茫心煎熬，奇蹟出現如珍寶。」
"As the living is uncertain my heart is suffering; As the miracle is appeared it looks like treasury"

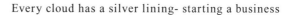

柳暗花明又一村─立業

Every cloud has a silver lining- starting a business

　　雖然命是保住了，還是要繼續與病魔搏鬥。因為我的病是慢性病，所以看病、吃藥需要持續很長的時間，不可能馬上就痊癒。人都很怕生病，就算得了病也要面對。生、老、病、死是每一個人的過程。我很年輕就得了重病，又是在我最需要賺錢的時候─每個月都要付房貸、還有兒女需要奶粉錢、父母親在農村也要生活費，我身上的責任非常重。想到這裡，總是感到非常的恐懼，每天無法安心的養病。有時候晚上不能入眠，想到這些事眼淚就會偷偷掉下來。雖然病情每天都有好轉，但進展卻是非常的緩慢，心急也沒有用，這種病就是要慢慢的去調養。療病期間，幾乎每天都要去看醫生和吃藥，這已經變成例行公事，覺得生病比貧窮更痛苦、更受煎熬。

　　Although my life had been saved, I had to continuously fight with the illness. My illness was a chronic disease, so I had to go to the doctor and took the medicine for a long time. It could not recover in a short period of time. People were afraid of diseases and we had to face it. Birth, death, illness, and growing old, is a process we all have to face. I got a serious disease when I was young and needed money the most. I had to pay the rent every month, my daughter needed milk money, and my parents lived on the farm need a living. I had huge responsibility and pressure. I felt scared when thinking of these and could not sleep well. I cried secretly sometimes. I felt better every day but the process was really slow. It was no use being hurry. This kind of disease had to be take care of nice and slow. During the recovering period, I had to see the doctor and took the medicine almost every day. These were like daily routines. Illness suffered more than being poverty.

在療病期間是沒辦法工作的，但每天家庭的開銷，還是需要支付，這總要想個辦法解決呀！雖然有一點點的積蓄，若沒有收入終究會坐吃山空。醫生又特別交代，不許過度勞累，要多休息、靜身養心。其實我自己心中有數，要很長一段時間無法工作。經過一年多的調養，才有辦法起身自由行動，雖然身體還是無法承受過度勞累，可是動腦筋去想事情已經不會造成太大的負擔。剛從台大醫院回來的時候，連過度的用腦想事情都會受不了，療養身心一年多，已經改善很多了。

I could not work during the nursing and recovering time but the expenses still had to be paid every day. I had to think of a solution. Though I still had some savings, I would be broke after all if I had no income. My doctor noticed me not to work too hard and remember to take a rest. I knew I could not work in this period. I could move normally after a year. My body could not afford too much tiredness, but to think and brainstorm would not be a big problem. When I just got back from the hospital, I could not over-use my brain. After a year of healing, I felt much better.

想來想去，真的不知所措。想到做自由業，那是最適合療養期間的身體狀況，但是我什麼經驗都沒有，這行不通，那行不通，只好每天看報紙想辦法。有一天看到報紙小廣告，裡面有買賣舊物品，還有中古機車、汽車、家庭電器，這些我也都不太懂。不過最後看到幾則賣舊房子的廣告最能吸引我的注意。心想，做這行買賣最適合我的體力狀況，一年買賣幾件就好了，又不會很勞累身體，這應該可以好好的研究吧！

I really did not know what to do. I wanted to be self-employed which was suitable for my situation but I had no experiences at all. I checked the newspaper every day and I saw an advertisement. It was about selling and buying used-goods, and there were motorcycles, cars, and electronics for sale. I did not know about marketing; however, there was an advertisement about selling old houses that caught my eyes. I thought that was suitable for me. Selling just a few houses a year could be enough and that should not be difficult. I could do some further studies on selling houses.

我做事比較保守。心想，買賣中古汽機車或家電比較複雜又會折舊。如果買來的中古屋賺不到錢或房子不好賣，那也可以租給人家收租金，補貼房屋的貸款支出，這樣比較沒風險。有了這個主意，我非常興奮。但是再仔細想，其實沒這麼美好。資金要從哪裡來？房子買賣金額龐大，資金才是真正的大問題，這對一個小市民來說算是龐大的金額，要如何籌措是件難事。如果沒有資金的來源，這個計劃也不用再想了。

I was rather conservative. I was wondering that selling old motorcycles, cars, or electronics could be complicated. If I could not sell the old houses or the prices was not good, I could rent the house and earn from the rent to pay my house loan. The risk would be lower. I was excited when having the idea but to think carefully, where did my funds come from? The price was huge for selling and buying houses so the funds became a big problem. It was a big amount for a little citizen. If I had no fund, the plan could not work.

挖盡心思，經過一段時間，結果皇天不負苦心人，讓我想到一個好辦法。我自己住的房子，幾年後已經成倍數漲價了，我可以跟銀行商量重新估價增貸。不夠的資金，可以標會。就依這個方法去籌劃。當時要向銀行貸款很困難，不容易貸到，利息又高（年利率18％）。我想盡辦法、全力以赴、只許成功、不可失敗。不到三個月，銀行批准我的增貸，我也標到了民間互助會。資金全部準備好，這樣就可以開始運作買賣中古屋。

I kept thinking of solutions. Finally I had an idea. The price of my house had raise after years, and I could talk with the banks to revaluate the loan. I could bid in the loan for the lack of funds.

I would raise my money this way. Back then, to loan from the bank was a difficult job and the interest was surprisingly high (the annual percentage rate: 18%). I tried so hard. After three months, the bank had accepted my loan-raise and I had bid the Rotating Saving and Credit Association (ROSCA). After the funds were ready, I could start to sell old houses.

從現在開始每天買二份報紙看售屋小廣告，以前賣房子皆登廣告，或張貼紅紙條在要出售房子的陽台上。我每天騎著機車到處尋找有要賣的房子，如果找到適當的房子，直接跟屋主議價，如果雙方談妥價格就成交，這是六十年代買賣不動產的交易方式，與九十年代買賣不動產有很大的差異，現今都是委託仲介來做不動產的買賣。

I started to buy two different newspapers for real estate ads. At that time, people posted ads on the newspaper for selling houses or put up red signs on the balcony saying the house was for sale. I rode my motorcycle along the streets searching for the houses for sale. I would discuss with the house owner when seeing a good house. If both sides had a good price the deal is done. This was how the real estate worked in the 60s, and it was very different from the 90s. Today most real estate transactions are done through agencies.

「明德學如端木賜，道心可應陶朱公。」
"The highest virtue learns as Ci Duanmu; the moral sense response as Li Fan"

從無到有——一步一腳印
From nothing to something- step by step

　　勤為無價珍寶，慎乃護身之術。買賣房子的過程很複雜，只要掌握住「勤」、「慎」二個原則，勤快的挑選物件與客戶，並且對於自己的權利小心謹慎，事實上會有不錯的成績。尤其我很幸運，有一位同鄉在當代書，這樣就可以請他幫我辦理過戶手續，也可以保障買方應有的權利，而且我又可以請教他全部代書業務的過程。不動產買賣非比一般，一定不能出一點差錯，否則一輩子無法翻身。我也很認真學習，買賣幾間後，就懂得過戶的流程。後來我就開始自己辦理不動產過戶手續。六十年代辦理自己的不動產過戶，本人就可以親自去地政事務所辦登記，不一定要有代書執照才能送件。只要了解程序，填好所有文件，就可以登記過戶。

　　The process of buying and selling the old houses was complicated. There were two basic principles to follow: diligent and cautious. Diligently choose my product and client, and be cautious about my own benefit could lead to a good performance. I am lucky to have a legal document writer who came from my hometown. He could help with my transfer registration and ensure the rights of the buyers. Selling and buying real estate were not like other businesses, I could not make any mistakes. Otherwise, it won't be easy to make up. I learned hard to know all steps of transferring after selling houses. After that I started to deal with transfer registration by myself. In the 60s, one could go to the conveyance office for the real estate transferring registration without a legal document writer's license. One just had to understand the procedure and filled-out the documents to register for a real estate transfer.

　　買來的中古屋一定要等到不動產過戶到我的名下，才可以推出銷售。以前買賣不動產的傳統觀念是－－「自己的不動產，自己買賣」，除非是親友介紹，不然不會透過第三者。來看房子的客人，都會先問，這個房子是你本人的嗎？如果告知不是自己的房子，他就立即離開，都不用再談。因此一定要過戶到我自己的名下，才可以推出銷售。

　　The old house that I bought had to be transferred under my name to sale. The concept of buying and selling the houses was "selling our own real estate". Therefore, we would not indirectly sale the houses through a third-person unless our relatives or friends introduced him or her. The clients would ask, "Is this your house?" If not, the client would leave and be unwilling to buy the house. This is why we had to transfer the houses under our names.

　　當時根本沒有仲介公司提供買賣服務，是到了七十年代，才開始有仲介公司開張服務。甚至七十年代早期，買賣不動產還是很少交給仲介。不動產交易金額很龐大，因此大家都很謹慎，不敢委託他人。隨著時代的變遷觀念，大眾的觀念也改變，現在的不動產幾乎都交給仲介公司買賣。

　　There were no real estate agencies at that time offering selling and buying service. In the 70s still a few real estate business would go through the agencies. People were very cautious about the real estate business and were afraid to trust others for selling, because the amount of the price was huge. However, as the generation changed, so did people's thought. The real estate today was all sell and buy through the agencies.

　　以前賣房子，一定要本人在場，這才能讓買方安心。我買進的房子，要先稍微整理，如粉刷油漆、換塑膠地板（以前公寓房子都是鋪塑膠地板或磨石子，不像現在全部鋪磁磚或櫸木地板），還要清洗得很乾淨，這會有很多的加分效果。除此之外，

要讓買房子的人對你印象好，因此簡介房子狀況時都要很誠實的
告知對方，當他對你有了信任，就有了交易機會。

When we sold houses, the house owner must be there in person
to be trusted by the buyer. After buying the house, I had to clean
the house, paint it, and rebuild the plastic floors (The houses were
paved with plastic or terrazzo floors, different from today's ceramic
tile or wooden floors). Redecorations help to add values to houses.
Moreover, I had to tell the house condition to the buyer honestly to
gain impression. While the buyer trusted you, there was the chance
of business.

以前大台北地區賣房子的方式，是將廣告板或紅紙條貼在要
賣的門前、菜市場或張貼在電線桿（在那個時候台北市電纜線還
沒地下化）、社區佈告欄。（以前張貼廣告，環保單位不會舉
發，因此只要明顯、適合的地方，都可以自行張貼，不像現在亂
張貼要罰幾千元。）不過效果最好的方式，還是在報紙刊登小廣
告。像這樣的工作，我做最適合，輕鬆又不勞累身體。當時還沒
有行動電話，我只能待在家裡等候。看了廣告後，對價格、地
點、坪數有興趣而想來看房子的人，都會先來電詢問，交談之
後，我們就約個時間去看房子。如果要出售的房子離我的家遠一
點，我白天就在現場等候買主來看房子，電話由家人接聽，請買
方直接到現場，才不用跑來跑去，也免得有時候我大老遠過去，
結果被放鴿子。

The old way of selling houses in Taipei city is to put up
boards and signs on the front gate, in the market, or on the electric
poles (The electric poles in Taipei city had not gone underground
yet) and community bulletin boards. (Posting advertisements
was not illegal at that time, and it would not be forbidden by the
Environmental Protection Agency. As long as the post was clear
and accurately posted, it was allowed to advertise.) However, the
best way to advertise and propagate is to put advertisements in the

newspapers. This was the best job for me because it was easy. We did not have cell phones so I would have to wait at home. People would call for some further information after seeing the ads if the price, place, and room size satisfied them. After discussing over phone, we would arrange a time to take a look at the house. If the house for sale was far from my house, I would wait at the selling house and my family would answer the phone calls. They would ask buyers to go directly to the selling house and I would not have to travel back and forth. This also avoided the cost of travelling a long way when the buyer didn't show up.

當時我買賣中古屋鎖定大台北地區，這也是正確的選擇。大台北地區人口多，需求也比較大，價錢相對就較高。即使到現在，大台北地區的房價，還是漲多跌少。因此，我當時正確的抉擇，使我賺了很多錢。我購買第一間中古屋總價六十萬元，一個月後，過戶完成，就開始整修，粉刷油漆，清洗得非常乾淨。整理完以後，就依照自己的想法推出去銷售。騎著摩托車到處貼紅紙條，還有刊登報廣告。報紙的售屋小廣告，費用不高，每天才一百多塊，雙管齊下，不到二個星期就以七十三萬賣掉，扣掉廣告，還有稅金，盈餘約十萬元。這和我原本的計畫相同，這次的交易，猶如吃了一粒定心丸，讓我對中古屋買賣的事業更有信心。也由於我的誠信，獲得了買方的信任，使得這次交易能夠順利完成。所以日後我所買賣中古屋的方式，均是依循此次交易的模式。

It was a right choice to focus on the old houses in Taipei city. It had a large population and that means a higher demand and a higher price. Even until now, the house price of Taipei city was still raising more than falling. Therefore, the right choice I made, earned me a lot of money. The first old second-hand house I bought was six hundred thousand dollars in total. After a month, when the transferring was done, I started to fix, paint, and clean it. Then I

sold the house according to my own way. I rode my motorcycle around posting red signs and putting up advertisements in the newspaper. It was not expensive to put ads for selling houses in the newspaper. It cost one hundred dollars a day. I sold the house for 7.3 hundred thousand dollars in two weeks. Deducted the cost of ads and the tax, I could get a hundred thousand dollars for profit. This was just like my plan. The deal had stronger my mind and I felt more confident in this business. My honesty had won the buyers trust and that made the deal successfully. From that on, I used the same method to sell houses.

「做事公正真仁義，賺得金錢心謙虛。」
"As business it's a real fair benevolence and righteousness; as earnings it's a modest kindness"

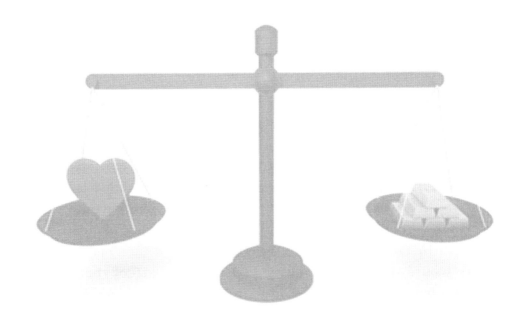

慢慢累積，漸漸穩定

Accumulate slowly to settle gradually

在買賣中古屋的過程中，多虧了長輩的指導，以及自己努力的學習，我很快就學會這方面的一切運作。幾年後又取得土地登記專業代理人證書，對我的工作更方便。

Thanks to some advises from the elders in the process of selling the old houses and my hard working, I soon understood the steps in the business. After a few years I got the license of professional land registration document writer. It was an advantage to my work.

做代書業務就是自由業，最適合我當時的身體狀況，又可以兼做買賣房子。所以說：待人恭敬，做事認真，腳踏實地，心存正念，自然會得到好報。今天的成果都是受到親朋好友的幫忙與照顧，我也一直抱持著感恩之心，當我做得非常順利的時候，一些親戚或朋友也會委託我替他們賣房子。但是我皆會據實以告，以當時的社會情況，不是在我名下的房子，要委託我賣，買方通常均會有所懷疑，如此一來，房子賣出機率相對降低。往往會白忙一場，徒勞無功。

Document writer is a freelance worker, it was good to my health and I could sell houses time to time. People would be well treated if they were nice to people, worked hard, and think positively. Thanks for my family and friends for what I had today, and I would always be thankful. Some of my friends would ask me to sell their houses because my work had gone successful. I would tell them the truth that if the house was not under my name, the buyers would doubt my honesty and it would affect the business. Also, my hard work would be in vain.

　　我本來想要開一家仲介公司，但當時看景氣不佳，房價好像在回檔。景氣不看好的時候，要買進中古屋，估價要非常的小心。每筆生意的交易金額均十分龐大，所以要斟酌盡善，不可以有一點差錯。否則一虧錢，財物損失慘重之外，精神上是會很痛心的。在三年半中，買賣幾十棟中古屋，也賺了幾百萬，除了家庭開銷費用，還盈餘了不少錢。在這段時間中，可以賺到錢，又可以療養身體，非常感激老天賜給我這個機運。三年來的調養，我的身體已完全康復。

　　I ought to open an agency but the economic seemed to fall. When the economic was decreasing, we had to be careful on valuing the house price when buying a old house. There could not be any mistake because the amount of the house price was huge, or else it would be a huge lost. I earned a few millions within three years from selling and buying old houses. Besides the expenses for family daily supplies, there was still much profit left. Thanks God for giving me the chance to recover and earn money at the same time. Three years of recovery heal my sickness and I got my health back to normal again.

　　中古屋買賣的過程，有一件事讓我確實的體悟到，即是人常說的｜「翻臉比翻書還要快」。事情的原委是這樣的，有一次買到一層公寓房子，所有權是兩人共有的，這兩位屋主原本是好朋友，兩人當場平分賣房子的房屋尾款。可是最後為了五千元費用，因認知上的不同，一直談不攏而最後翻臉。為了讓事情圓滿結束，我提議這五千元由我支付，才讓這件事尷尬收場。當時我只是不想讓兩位好友因錢而變成仇人，而花了這筆不應該由買方支付的錢。可是到最後我並沒有吃虧，因為現在想起那幾年買賣三十幾棟中古屋，賺最多錢就是那一間房子，這可能也是種好因的結果吧！

During the process of buying and selling the old houses, I realized how people get angry easily. I once bought a house owned by two people. The two owners were good friends, and they split the balance. Unfortunately, they had different thoughts about five thousand dollar payment and could not come to a conclusion then they turned against each other. In order to end it up, I suggested that I paid the five thousand dollars. I did not want these two good friends to become enemies because of this money so I paid for what I didn't have to pay. However I did not loss anything, because that house made the most money of all among thirty houses I sold. That might be the gain of good causes I plant.

「誠實謙恭做生意，交易公平合情理。」
"I do business with honesty and modesty; the
business trade is fair and reasonable"

失敗成功一線間

There's just one line between failure and success

撇步—買賣中古屋的五項要訣
Tips – five knacks to buying and selling old houses

　　在這一次的買賣當中，我體悟到自己的想法是正確的：買賣對人要謙虛、恭敬、實在。全部屋況的資料向買方詳細的告知，不得隱瞞。開始要給買方建立誠實的印象。不動產交易金額龐大，每個人都會很謹慎，也因此要先讓買方信任賣方，覺得這個人是有誠信的，這才有可能再進一步商量交易價格。買不動產時許多人幾乎全家出動，來回看好幾趟才能下訂金，因此更需要具備十足的耐心，要能不厭其煩的帶買方看屋和解說。

　　I realized that my thought was right for this business deal: be humble, respect, and honest to others. We have to tell the entire house status to the buyer without hiding anything. It was important to set an honest impression to the buyers. Everybody was careful and cautious because the dealing price of the real estate was really huge. Therefore we had to be trusted by the buyers to talk about price in the next step. People mostly came in with family to look around the houses for times to assure on paying the initial payment. In this case I had to be more patient to show the buyers around the house and answer all questions.

　　買房子是一件非常重要的事情，想到有的人辛苦賺錢，一輩子只為買一棟房子能夠安居，而省吃儉用，所以我對買方會更加用心。我都建議客人多考慮再決定，才不會買到不喜歡或不適合的。這也是人常說：做事憑良心，就是道德。尤其像買房子這種大事，務必要保護他的權利。做生意要待人真誠，先想到他人的利益，這會讓人家感到我待人真心。如果成交，我會感到高興又心安。

Buying a house is a very important event. Some people made efforts to earn money and tried so hard to save money just to buy a house to live in comfort for their whole life. Thus I will devote my heart to the buyers. I suggested buyers to consider over and over again to make sure not to buy a house they did not like or unsuitable. Do things with morality. Especially when it came to buying a house, I must protect the right of the buyers. Be honest in doing business and the buyer's right is always the priority. These would show my honesty to the buyers. If the deal was made, I would feel happy and carefree.

我遇到幾個買方,他們都說:「我聽你講話很實在,看你不會有欺人之心,因此比較安心買你這間房子。」所以一開始就要建立誠信是正確的。帶買方看房子要提醒自己:一、廢話不說。二、屋況真實告知買方。三、承諾的事一定要做到。四、絕對不能讓買方覺得你說話顛三倒四。五、要給買方感受到大家好像是朋友。做買賣說話要忠誠守信,行事要敦厚恭敬。誠信是成功之本,一個人只要真誠的待人處事,就會容易獲得他人的好感和信任。我依照這樣的模式買賣中古屋。有的一間房子只賺幾萬元,但是有幾間利潤好一點,賺了幾十萬也有。只要有賺錢就出售,這樣就可以很快來回買賣,到後來賺到了錢就可以同時買二間房子了。

I met a few buyers and they all said, "You seemed honest and should not lie or take advantages, therefore we feel safe to buy your house." Building honesty and trust in the beginning was a right thing to do. When showing the house to the buyers, I reminded some key points to myself: not to talk much, tell the truth about the house, do what I have promised, never be incoherent or confused the buyers, and be friends with the buyers. Be honest when doing the business and respect others. Honest is the key to success. One must be true to others, to be trusted by others. I followed the keys in the business. Some of the houses made only a few ten thousands, and some made more profits like hundred thousand. If the price met my goal, I would sell the house. This could speed up the business, and in the end I could buy two houses at a time.

「成功需要更積極，膽大心細須用意。」
"It needs more active for success; it needs an intent
look with bold stroke and carefulness"

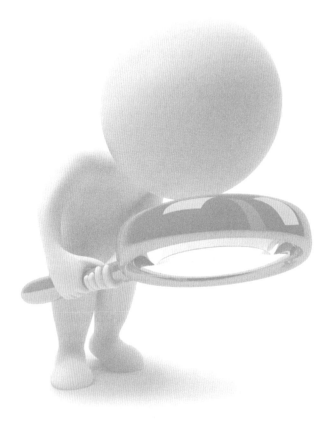

負面教材─取捨之間

The negative material – between choices

　　中古屋買賣並不是穩賺不賠的生意，能賺錢的主要因素，是需要具備獨到的眼光和當機立斷的決心。舉個真人真事的例子，我有一位朋友，他家境很不錯，也很努力經營事業。有一天他繼承父母的遺產，得到價值超過一億的不動產。他的個性算節儉，人又聰明，雖然這些錢他並沒有自己用掉，可是不到十年就如黃粱一夢，一無所有了。

　　Buying and selling the old houses was not an easy business. The reason why I could earn money was that I got special insight and a determination. As an example from a true story, I have a friend who came from a poor family but he worked very hard. One day he inherited all the money from his parents, and got a real estate worth several hundred million dollars. He was very frugal and smart. Even though he did not spend all the money on himself, the money was all gone within ten years.

　　事情的經過是這樣的，我這位朋友認為自己很聰明，想要買賣不動產來賺取價差。所以選在台北縣中和地區買了一間大店面，並向銀行貸款八千萬，而且又向民間借了二千萬。可是買了之後，不動產開始走下坡，這當然就賺不到差價。剛開始還有人出價要買，可是要賠三百萬元；再隔半年又有人出價，即使賣掉也要賠六百萬元。他心想我是買來賺差價的，哪有可能虧錢賣掉，所以不賣。

　　This was how the story goes: My friend thought he was smart and wanted to buy houses to earn money from the overcharge. He bought a store in Chungho, Taipei County, and loaned eighty million dollars from the bank. Also, he borrowed twenty million dollars from a non-governmental organization. However, the price started to fall after he had bought the house. He apparently could not earn the overcharge. People still called the price and wanted to buy the house at the beginning but he would loss three million dollars. After six months, people called the price for the house but he would have to loss six million dollars. He thought he was going to earn from the overcharge, not to lose money, so he refused to sell the house.

　　不動產一直不漲，持續了將近七年。當時銀行年利息一點零五分，民間利息二至三分，總共加起來每個月要付一百多萬的利息。他繼承的那些公寓房子，就一間一間的賣掉來付利息，不到七年的時間，就賣掉所有的房子。在這七年期間總共付掉近一億元的利息。然而，景氣持續低迷，當時就算賣掉房子，所得的價錢也不夠還欠銀行的錢，更沒有能力再付利息了。所以到最後店面被銀行拍賣掉，更慘的是拍賣的錢尚不夠還給銀行，變成銀行的債務人。（房子被銀行拍賣掉的金額不夠償還銀行，剩餘欠的錢還是要還清為止，不然會成為所有金融、銀行的拒絕往來戶，成為「信用破產」的人。）

　　The price of the real estate would not rise for almost seven years. The interest rate at the bank was 1.05% a year and the interest rate for some non-governmental organizations were 2 to 3%. So the interest was about a hundredth of several hundred million a month in total. The apartment houses that he inherited were sold house by house to pay for the interests. He had sold all his houses not until seven years. He had paid almost one hundred million interests in the seven years. However the economic was still in a depression. Even if he sold all the houses, the money he earned would not be enough for paying the money he owned the banks. In addition, he could not afford the interests anymore. In the end, the bank had sold his store. The worst thing was that the money was still not enough for returning the bank. He had become the debtor of the bank. (The bank sold the house but the amount of the money was not enough to pay back the bank. The money had to be paid off or else one would be blocked by all banks and became credit-broken.)

這個例子主要在說明，我這位朋友由於他的個性太任性、固執，再加上放不下，最後導致終生遺憾。這是投資房地產買賣的大忌，沒有獨到的眼光與當機立斷的決心，實在不適合從事這個行業。

This story tells that my friend was too stubborn and unwilling to let things go, so he lives his life in regret. This was a taboo to the investors in the house selling and buying business. One was not suitable for the business without special insight and determination.

現在是多元化的社會，需要多聞、多問，就能得到很多不一樣的訊息、觀點和建議，又能增長智慧，尤其是在緊要關頭的時候，更需要懂得去請教他人。每個人的工作、行業都不一樣，所以集思廣益，對自己一定有好處的。最怕的是堅持己見，認為自己很了不起，最後卻失去了不該失去的。

The society is now multicultural. People need to know and ask more to acquire different information, aspects, and suggestions. Especially in the very key moment, we have to ask for help. People have different jobs; therefore, collecting useful ideas from various aspects would definitely be a benefit. We must avoid sticking to one's opinion and being proud, because that would lead to a great loss.

當自己有一點積蓄時，一定要謹慎理財。如有快速賺錢的捷徑，一定要更加小心！這未嘗不是賭的一種方式，來的快，去的也快，這是絕對的。切莫心存僥倖去嘗試！所謂一步一腳印，凡事按部就班，時常警惕自己，不要過於相信賺錢有捷徑。否則當血本無歸時，想後悔時已太晚了！我做事都會先衡量自己的能力，然後再去做。即使失敗了，還有機會翻身。千萬不要像我這位朋友，他這一生再也沒有機會了。

When you have some savings, remember to manage your money well. If there are some shortcuts to earn money fast, you must be extremely careful. That was unlikely to be a way to bet. It comes fast and gone fast for sure. Be sure not to take advantages and be practical. Do things orderly and be attentive. Do not trust the shortcuts of earning money or it would be too late to cry over spilled milk. I would judge my own ability before doing things. Even though I failed, I would still have a chance to start over. Never be like this friend of mine, having no chances to regret.

「謹慎理財成寶坊，集思廣益有義方。」
"If it managed finances carefully it could be a treasury; if it collected opinions widely it could be a benefit"

成功是用「心」換來的

Exchanging success with a heart of diligence

　　行萬里路、勝讀萬卷書。經驗是書本上學不到的，唯有親身經歷過，才會真正的瞭解其珍貴。就好比經營事業，經驗越多，越能應付各種不同的狀況。很多年以前我買到一間超便宜的房子，而且是有人先付訂金，因為賣方不肯馬上過戶給買方，最後買方不敢買而解約。這個房子跟我住處都在同一棟公寓，房東要賣房子我本來並不知情，是他的房客告知我的。我與那位房客平常遇到都會打招呼或寒暄幾句，有一天他告訴我他的房東已賣掉房子，他可能很快就會搬家了。可是經過一星期後那位房客又說因為雙方談不攏而解約了，他也不知道原因，可是房東好像急需賣掉這間房子。其實我以前就對這間房子有興趣，所以請房客約時間帶我去見房東。過了幾天我和房東見了面，我們聊了一下，我就瞭解了整件事的來龍去脈，為何會解約的原因。

Knowledge comes from books and from experiences of the world. Experience is what you cannot learn from books. Only experiencing in person could one know the true meanings. That is just like doing business. With more experiences, people could handle various possible troubles. Years ago I bought an inexpensive house and the prepayments of the house were already paid. Due to the seller would not transfer to the buyer immediately, so the buyer refused to buy the house and cancelled the contract. The house was in the same apartment as mine and the seller's guest told me about the house. The guest and I would do some daily conversations when we met in the neighborhood. One day he told me that his landlord had sell the house so he had to move soon. However the guest said the buyer had cancelled the contract because they could not make a deal and he did not know why. The landlord seemed in a hurry to sell the house. In fact I was interested in buying the house for a long time so the guest took me to meet his landlord. A few days later I met the landlord and I knew the reason why they broke the contract after having a small talk with the landlord.

　　因為這個房子登記為出租屋，又讓房客設戶籍，所以賣方的增值稅不能享有自用住宅的稅率，只能用一般稅率計算，是自用住宅的十倍，需要繳一百六十萬元，如果是自用住宅稅率只要繳十六萬元。問題是房客的戶籍設在這間房屋的地址，必須要等房客的戶籍遷出一年之後，該房子才能申報成自用住宅。因此賣方想要等一年後，才將房子過戶給買方。如此一來，他就可以省下一百四十四萬元。然而，對買方而言，若是賣方收了錢，一年後又不履行過戶的承諾，買方豈不血本無歸。即使買方相信賣方的為人，但所謂天有不測風雲、人有旦夕禍福。若在這一年中，賣方有所不測，買方又該怎麼辦呢？像這種條件，一般買方都不會接受，不僅風險太大了，而且也不合常理。

The house had registered as a rented house but at the same time it opened up a household registration. Thus the buyer's value added tax could not count as the tax rate of a living house. It could only be counted as regular tax and the regular tax was ten times the living house tax (one million six hundred thousand dollars). The living house tax cost only one hundred and sixty thousand dollars. The problem was that the guest's household address set on the house would change to a living house one year after they moved out. Therefore the seller had to wait one year to transfer the house to the buyer and the seller could save one million four hundred and forty thousand dollars. However, to the buyer, it would be a risk if the seller got the money and broke the promise after one year. Even if the buyer trusted the seller, there are always some unpredictable problems. What should the buyer do if the seller had an accident? Buyers would not accept occasions like this. Not only it was too risky, but too unreasonable.

見了面之後，屋主有意將房子便宜一百萬賣給我，最後他提出的條件也是要等一年再過戶給我。因為他急需要用這筆錢，我立刻就決定買下來，因為我知道如何保護自己的權利。房子總價五百六十萬，雙方訂定契約，我先付四百萬，剩餘金額一百六十萬等明年過完戶再一次付清。付頭期款同時，房子就點交給我，所以馬上當現成的房東了。

After I met the landlord, he intended to sell the house to me for one million dollars. Eventually his condition was to transfer the house to me after one year. Since he needed the money very badly, I had decided to buy the house immediately and knew how to protect my rights. The total price of the house was five million six hundred thousand dollars. We agreed and signed the contract then I prepaid four million dollars. The one million six hundred thousand dollars balance would be paid after the transfer next year. The house was mine after I paid the down payment and I was the landlord.

一旦雙方訂了契約，就要依照契約來履行。可是如果賣方在這一年當中或之前向民間借錢沒還，債權人隨時可以提出查封房子之訴訟，因為所有權還是屬於原屋主的，如果被查封拍賣，我可能就分不到錢。問題來了，這要如何才能夠保障我「買方」的權利呢？我的作法是在雙方訂定契約時，由我提出要求，在我付頭期款的「當天」，賣方必須把其不動產，辦理設定抵押權四百萬給我。依照「債權是依順序保障」的法則，即使在一年內房子尚未過戶給我，若被查封拍賣，由於我排在第一順位，我絕對不會有損失。因此做哪一行都要認真、細心、用心、多聞、多問，對自己一定有好處，這次交易能順利成功，其原因就是在此。

As soon as the contract has signed, we must follow the contract. If the seller had not paid off the money borrowed from a non-governmental organization, the creditor could always propose an action to seal up the house. The ownership has belonged to the house owner. Once the house was sealed up and been sold, I could not get any money. Here comes the problem, how do I protect my buyer's rights? My way was to make a request when signing the contract: on the day I pay the down payment, the seller had to conduct the mortgage of his real estate to me in four million dollars. According to the law, "the creditor's right is protected in orders". That is, even if others did not transfer the house to me in one year and the house had been sealed and sold, I was in the first order so I will not suffer any loss. Therefore we must be really careful no matter which business we are in. Being careful, knowledgeable, and ask more, would definitely an advantage. These were the reasons that my business could have gone so well.

「敦親睦鄰貴人到，誠懇待人有福報。」
"If it be a good neighbor the mentor comes; if it is sincere for people the karmic reward will be received"

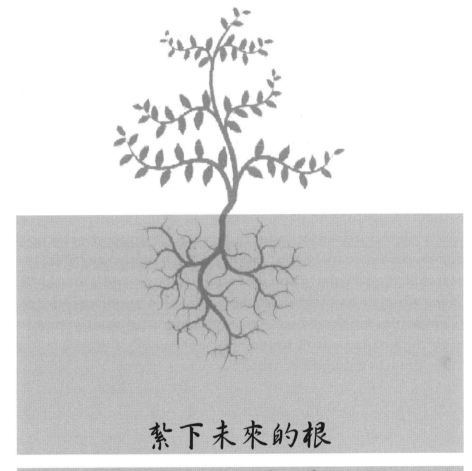

紮下未來的根

Planting for the future

山不轉路轉—高科技產業的先行者
There's always a way – the pioneer of the high tech

　　民國六十九年開始，景氣不好，持續到七十一年。在這二年我幾乎停止買賣中古屋，雖然有土地登記專業代理人證書，可以做代書業務，可是我剛出道，沒有客源，賺的錢不夠家庭開銷。心想這行現在景氣不佳，若一味的苦撐下去，絕對會坐吃山空，我還是要另謀出路。

Since the 69th year of the Republic Era, the economic had been in a depression until the 71th year. I stopped selling the old houses in these two years. Though I had the certificate of professional land registration document writer and I could be a document writer, I had just start the business without customers or guests. Thus the money I earn was not enough for family supplies. I though the business was tough. If I continued, I would not get anything. I must find another way.

　　剛好在這段休息期間，有親戚提起電子遙控之事，說現在這行利潤很好。但是我對電子一竅不通，什麼交流電、直流電、110伏特、220伏特，我完全不懂，要如何去做這行業呢？不過由於之前買賣中古屋順利，確實有賺到一些錢，再加上身體又康復了，雖然對遙控這行不懂，但是我卻興緻勃勃的。遙控這個名詞在當時聽起來非常的新穎，又是高科技，這個行業對我而言是一個非常大的挑戰。

During my recuperation, a relative had brought up something about electronic remote controllers and it brought good profits. I knew nothing about electronics: AC (alternating current), DC (direct current), 110 volts, and 220 volts. I knew nothing and how would I start the business? Due to the former successful business of selling the houses, I did earn some money. Plus, my health went back again so I became excited about the remote control business I am not so good at. The word "remote control" sounds new, and it was high-tech. The business was a big challenge to me.

　　經過幾個月的思考研究，第一步該如何進行？結果想出一個方法，就是請人幫我設計。但是當時懂得這種技術的人並不多，甚至可以說是非常的少，也很難找得到。況且那時台灣也還沒有網際網路，不像現在打開電腦要找任何事物應有盡有。所以，我請親友幫忙打聽懂電子的人才。經過一段時間，有位朋友介紹一位正在做玩具喇叭外銷的人給我認識。見面之後感覺還不錯，他說他有能力設計，並且可以生產遙控器交由我來銷售。就這樣很順利地找到了我需要的人了。不過，他要求先付四萬元給他去買電子零件，以便開發設計。

　　By a few months of thinking and studying, where should I start? I came up an idea: find someone to design for me. However, at that time, there were few people who know the skills, and they were difficult to find. In addition, there was no Internet, unlike today that we could find anything on the web. I asked my friend to help looking for someone who understands electronics. Time passed, a friend introduced a toy horn exporter to me. I had a good impression on him after we met. He said he had the ability to design and could produce remote control for me to sell. Luckily I found whom I needed but he asked for forty thousand dollars for the electronic components in developing his design.

　　幾個月後，他宣稱開發成功，又要我付四十幾萬去買更多的電子零件來開始生產。這次要付的金額比較多，由於我不懂技術和生產，當然要信任他，從沒想過他會心懷不軌。結果，他交給我的竟是一些遙控玩具，根本不是我要的產品。後來才知道他根本也不懂技術，又怎可能生產？那些遙控其實是他買來搪塞我的，於是我就這樣被騙了四十四萬元。經過此番的挫折，也讓我長了一番見識。有了這一次的經驗，我再找合作對象就更加小心了。

The exporter claimed that he had successfully developed the products and asked for four hundred thousand dollars to buy more electronic components. I had to pay a large amount this time but I knew nothing about the skills and producing. Thus, I choose to trust him without any doubts. Eventually he handed me some remote-controlled toys, which were completely different from what I want. Actually he did not know about any skills, so how did he produce? Those toys were just excuses to fob me off. I had been robbed for four hundred and forty thousand dollars. This frustrating event has taught me a lesson and increased my knowledge. After this experience, I would be more careful next time when finding someone to work with.

「嘔心瀝血望進財，美玉勞日琢磨來。」
"It takes infinite pains for earnings; it carves
and polishes for beautiful jade"

失敗為成功之母

Failure can lead to success

　　不經一事，不長一智。雖然被騙了四十幾萬，我對繼續開發遙控產品，還是充滿了信心。不過，這次我就謹慎的擬定幾個方案。首先，雙方務必簽訂契約，才能保障彼此的權利。不要再像上次因為信任對方，沒訂契約才上當受騙。此次重整旗鼓，再接再厲。幾個月後，有位朋友介紹一位開發設計師給我。兩人初見面，感覺他非常優秀。但為免重蹈覆轍，經過友人介紹及自己的深入了解，知道該設計師是台北工專電子科畢業。

Practice makes perfect. Although I had been fraud four hundred dollars, I was still confident in developing remote controlling products. I would be more careful when making up my minds. First, we must signed contracts for our rights or else I would be cheated like last time just because I trusted others so much. I had everything now and was ready to start. A few months later, a friend of mine introduced a develop designer to me. I considered him an outstanding man when seeing him at first sight. To avoid making the same mistake, I met the man for further understanding. The designer was graduated from National Taipei Institute of Technology(NTIT).

　　當時電子科系畢業的人才並不好找到，加上這次我非常的謹慎，一開始我就先設定二個階段：開發設計一個階段，生產為另一個階段，採用二段式的合作，條件則由他先提出來討論。他要求第一階段開發費用五萬元，等到產品達到我的標準後，第二階段才開始生產符合我要的產品，一組二千八百元，每次最少訂購100組。這種合作方式兩人都同意，我要先付開發費用五萬元，如果達不到我要的功能，就要退還五萬元；如果成功，再繼續合作進行第二階段。我想,按照這種合作方式,即使失敗或被騙,最多也只損失五萬元,所以我很放心地委託他設計。

At that time, it was not easy to meet anyone graduated from the electronics department of National Taipei Institute of Technology. I was really careful this time so I set two level steps: developing and design as one step, and producing as another step. For the two-step cooperation, he could propose the price for discussion. He asked for fifty thousand dollars in the first step. When the products reached my standard quality, the second step could start producing products. The price was two thousand and eight hundred dollars a set, and the orders were 100 sets at least. We both agreed on this kind of cooperation. I would pay fifty thousand dollars first for development. If the function did not reach my standard quality, I would have to take back fifty thousand dollars. As soon as the first step was successfully developed, we could go on to the second step. I thought that even though this kind of cooperative relation failed or I got fraud, it would be at most fifty thousand dollars. Therefore I gave the design job to the man without worrying.

契約開發期限一個月,他準時交出第一台遙控讓我測試,測試結果,遙控的功能符合我的要求。接下來,我們就進行第二階段的合作模式,開始依照合約生產100組,這也是我要傷腦筋的時候。他生產給我的只是組件基板加初步測試,然而要從零件組合變成一樣正規可以使用的產品,再交到客人手上,還必需有塑膠模具、安裝說明書、使用功能說明書、外觀包裝、保證書。

The contrast period for developing was one month. He handed in his first remote control on time for me to test. The result of the testing showed that the remote control had reached my request. Then we could process the second step. The contrast said to produce 100 sets at first. This is what I am worried about. What the designer gave me were just basic testing of modules and substrates.

There should be plastic models, installing instructions, using instructions, packing, and product guarantee to form a complete usable product for customers.

　　還有一件重要的事，如果產品全部做好，一切完備，要如何推銷？我要做的事情怎麼一下子變得這麼多？到此時才深刻體悟到，從生產出一樣產品，賣到使用者手上，要花多少心血。生產後販賣，這樣的生意比買賣中古屋複雜得多。

　　There was one important thing. How did we market the product after the products were all set? How come I have to do so many things at once? I suddenly realized how much should one devote to produce one product into the consumers' hands? The selling after production sounded more complicated than selling the old houses.

「宏偉前途自創造，失敗成功心常照。」
"The magnificent prospects could be created by one's own; it is always illuminated with the mind of success and failure"

為公司命名
Naming a company

「小心百事可做，大意寸步難行」。當時我首先要面對的最大問題，是公司只有我自己一個人。

You could do everything with a careful heart but careless could ruin everything. The biggest problem that I had to confront was that I was the only person in my company.

新開一家公司，其實可以聘請很多人幫我工作，但我心想，請人做事要付薪水呀！我也不是有錢人家的子弟，剛開始做生意，當然要先自己一個人動手，這叫做「一人公司」。有了業績再聘請技術員來共事，一步一腳印按部就班地創業，如果失敗也不會損失很多金錢。

When opening a company, I should hire people to work for me. I had to pay for the workers and I was not raised in a rich family. Thus I was on my own when beginning a business. This was called a "one person company". I would hire some technician after I had accomplished a business achievement. I would not loss too much money if I do things orderly.

我從年輕就辛苦賺錢，即使現在有一點積蓄，也是努力工作，加上省吃儉用，才存下來的。縱然現在我開公司了，我還是要勤奮並且謹慎的去做。天下萬事本非易，人就是要不斷的突破困境以成長。

I worked hard to earn money since I was young. I cut expenses to have some savings today. Even though I established my own company, I worked really hard and careful. Things were not simple from the beginning, so we have to overcome the difficulties to become mature.

　　生產加販賣一定要先成立一家公司。公司命名路特，英文ROOT，中文的意思是「根」。路特的由來，是以ROOT的中文譯音而命名，主要靈感是來自於當時有一部小說改編成的電影「根」。內容是敘述一位美國黑人，要了解他的祖先是從何處來到美國，又是怎麼來的。這段尋根的過程以及黑人在異國受到的不平等待遇，都描述得十分詳細，受到全世界的人讚賞。當然，我也是深深被這部電影所感動。於是我將公司命名為「根」，是想表達對美國黑人致敬。

One must establish a company to produce and sell. I named my company "Lu-te". It was the sound of "Root" in English, meaning the start and the core of things. The name came from the novel-adopted movie "Root". It was about an African American searching for clues about where and how did his ancestors come to America. The story talked about how the African American been discriminated and unfairly treated while finding his "root". The story was praised for how detail and delicate it described the story. Of course, I was influenced and touched by the movie as well. Therefore, I named my company "Root" to pay tribute to the African Americans.

　　天下無難事，只怕有心人。設立公司需要五個人當股東，我的五個股東都是自己的親人，還要先存入銀行最少一百萬元當做資本額（還好我當時買賣中古屋賺的錢都存起來，所以現在準備申請成立公司的資金，對我來說輕而易舉），然後再請會計師送件申請公司執照和營業執照。有了這兩張執照，就可以到稅捐處申請發票，做生意一定要開出發票，才是正規營運。因公司執照、營業執照和發票都準備好了，這就可以正式營業。

Nothing is impossible to a willing mind. A company needs five shareholders and five of my shareholders were all relatives. I also needed to put one million dollars in the bank as capital (Thank God that I save all the money earned from selling the old houses, so it was easy for me to apply the capital for establishing a company.) After that, I would have my accountant to send the application for company license and business license. Having both licenses, I could apply for the receipt. We have to give receipt when doing business as a proper operation. A company could run officially when having company license, business license, and receipt.

申請執照，同時也規劃生產，雙管齊下，才可以節省時間。現在我每天要做的事情真的很多，一大早開始到晚上十二點忙個不停，一天工作十幾個小時。產品要有商標才能取信於客人，註冊是保證、商標是責任，這是我做生意堅持的理念。要提出申請商標著作權，先要設計想擁有的商標圖案和文字。請人設計要花錢，自己做可省掉。我想到一位朋友他女兒讀美工設計，就請她幫忙畫了幾個圖案給我看。我給她三個圖案的要件做參考，一部汽車、一扇鐵捲門，以及英文字母ROOT。結果她畫了三張很漂亮的圖檔給我，我把汽車還有鐵捲門的圖放入Ｒ字的框裡面，心想這可以表示好幾個意思：

一、Ｒ是真實ＲＥＡＬ（反璞歸真）。

二、英文ROOT的字母Ｒ代表中文路特公司。

三、在車上可以遙控鐵捲門，車和鐵捲門兩個圖案全部放進Ｒ框裡面。

四、整個圖案的下方是英文ROOT。

那個時代高級的產品都是外國貨，所以商標、廠牌都寫上英文。當時遙控器算高科技也是高級產品，因此我就把英文字印在遙控器正面和外面包裝上。有了這樣的標示，產品比較好賣。朋友和客人都稱讚這個商標好看又特殊。

Meanwhile when applying for the licenses, I scheduled the

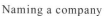

products to save time. I had a lot of things to do every day from early morning to twelve at night. My products had to have a trademark to win the trust from the customers. The registration was a guarantee and the trademark was responsibility. This is my concept of business. One must design a logo to apply for the right of the trademark. It cost money to hire people for designing the logo so it would be better to do it on my own. I thought of a daughter of my friend who studied art design. I asked her to design a few picture and gave her three pictures as references: a car, a rolling shutter, and the English word "root". She designed three beautiful pictures for me. I put the picture of the car and the gate in the circle of the letter "R" and thought that would indicate so many meanings:

1. R is for "real",

2. The letter R stands for the company "Root" (Lu-te),

3. The rolling shutter could be remote-controlled from the car, and the picture of both the car and the gate were in the circle of the letter R,

4. The word "Root" was beneath the picture.

At that time, the fancy products were imported from other countries, so the trademarks and the brands were in English. The remote control was a high-class and high-tech product; thus I put the English word on both the remote control and the packing. The products would sell better with the sign like that. My friends and customers were all complimenting on the nice and special trademark.

「註冊商標是保證，服務品質是責任。」
"A registered trademark is promised; a quality
of service is responsibility"

慘澹經營的草創期

The beginning of the gloomy operation

有了商標著作權證書，就要開始準備印刷信封、貼紙、包裝材料、紙箱，還有外觀設計。產品附屬零件，螺絲、線材、外殼等等，全部自己一個人想辦法做好，真的馬不停蹄。在半年之內，我就做好必須要完成的工作。我很認真去了解，有不會的就請教長輩或專業的人。半年之後，產品也正式小量生產，我就要更積極去推展產品了。

After I had the right certificate of the trademark, I should start preparing for envelopes, stickers, packing materials, boxes, and packing designs. I was in charge of the materials attached to the products: screws, wires, and the packing covers. I did what I have to do in six months and tried hard to understand the business by asking the elders or the professionals. After six months, the products were produced a little amount and I needed to promote my products more actively.

當時還沒有行動電話，所以要請一位工讀生幫我接電話，這樣薪水開支比較低。其實剛開始我對遙控器安裝也不熟悉，遙控器是要控制鐵捲門上升、下降、停止的功能，一定要和鐵捲門馬達結合才能達到遙控的效果。我是半路出家，對電路一竅不通，推銷起來會很辛苦，因此要特別用心。

We did not have cell phones at that time so I needed a part time worker to pick up the phones for saving salary expenses. In fact I was unfamiliar with installing remote controls at first. The remote control was for the rolling shutter to go up and down or pause. It must be linked to the motor in the rolling shutter to control the shutter remotely. I was an amateur of the electronics so it was difficult to promote the products.

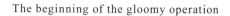

　　皇天不負苦心人，讓我想到有效的推銷好方法，就是每次外出推展業務，都攜帶一樣禮品去拜訪客人。禮品不可以寒酸，我準備的是幾百塊錢的餅乾禮盒，適合小孩也適合大人（當時這樣的禮品算是很體面）。初見面攜帶禮品拜訪客人，客人就有不同的感受，也給了他一個好的印象。有了好印象，我們還希望談生意彼此能相契合，就要先順著客人話題和他聊天，以他為中心，千萬不可打斷他。這樣談生意之事等他提出再談，或留在最後再介紹產品，雖然是第一次見面，談到最後兩人猶如相識很久。有人常說：不是得到就是學到，我全部都得到了。

　　The heaven will not disappoint the person who tries. I found a good way to promote my products. I brought gifts to visit my guests or customers every time when I go out for business. We could not be cheap on gifts. I bought hundred-dollars cookie gift boxes that were suitable for both children and adults (the gift like this was very decent and respectable at that time). The customers would feel different when receiving gifts at first sight with good impression. With good impression, we hope to have a pleasant business conversation. We follow the topic of our customers to keep on the conversation and could not interrupt our customers. We waited until the customers proposed the business topic or left the product introduction to the last. Though we had seen each other for the first time, it seemed like we have known each other for a long time at the end of the conversation. There is a saying goes: "if you did not gain it, you must learn it", and I had gained everything.

　　一般客人會先介紹他現在正在使用的品牌功能有多好，我就趁勢去了解其他廠牌的功能，並且和自己的遙控器互相比較。這樣不但能更了解市場的需求，也可激起求進步的企圖心。千萬記住，不言同行是非少敵人，多了解同行產品最聰明，不可批評他牌產品的不是，要很客氣的說：「請試用我的產品，也是一樣好用。價錢我們好商量。」

Customers would usually first introduce the advantages of the brand they were using, and then I would take the opportunity to understand the function of other brands. Also, I would compare my own products with others. I could understand the market needs and would have the motivation to keep progressing. But keep in mind that we do not criticize or claiming right or wrong of others. It was a smart way to understand products from the same field and avoid criticizing other brands. We had to say in a polite way, "Please try my products. The quality is equally good and the price is discussible."

遙控器是有一定的價位，他也不會亂殺價，這樣有技巧地引導他出價，就有機會做到生意。有時候他要展現自己很內行，來考我一些技術上的問題，我就順著這個機會請教他，他也會很樂意的教我，這樣兩個人就變成朋友了。每次去拜訪一定攜帶一樣禮品，經過幾次見面談話，大約了解他的嗜好，喜歡抽煙或喝酒以及喜歡什麼品牌，下次就送他喜愛的東西。不管禮物多或少，一般的人收到都會感受到溫馨。

There was a standard price for the remote controls so customers would bargain within a reasonable range. I technically guided customers to come up with a price, and I would have the chance to make money. Sometimes customers would ask technical questions to show how professional they are, and I would take the advantage to learn from them. The customer would be glad to teach me some knowledge then we would become friends. I would bring gifts every time I pay a visit. After a few times visiting and conversation, I understood their hobbies (smoke, or drink) or favorite brands. I would bring the gifts they like next time I paid a visit. No matter how much gifts, they would be happy to get them and felt warm.

「推展業務笑臉開，專心經營財神來。」
"It is always smile for promoting business; if it can focus on business then Mammon comes"

發展營運的關鍵—維持和客戶的好關係

The essential elements of developing a business- maintain a good relationship with the customers

　　會想到送禮，是我前二年去日本旅行時，了解到他們的習俗，如果店家要賣東西，經常會送個小禮物給客人，讓人感到窩心，這種社交禮儀運用在我的生意上最好不過。全省各地區，經過一個多月拜訪客人，大致有不錯的成果。

The reason why I came up with the idea of giving gifts was from the times that I went to Japan two years ago. I understood their customs that the shops would give small gifts to the customers and they would feel warm and sweet. This social manner would be best for my business. I visited guests all around the country and having great results.

　　雖然有的還沒下訂單，但是我給客人有好的印象，以後就會有希望做到生意（有燒香有保佑）。雖然有的客人安裝遙控器不多，但是也很熱心介紹他的下游廠商，來購買我的遙控器。像這種推薦方式，十之八九都會做到生意。

Even though some customers had not request an order yet, they had good impressions on me for further businesses. Some customers did not set up many remote controls but they introduced more customers to me. This kind of recommendation business would mostly success.

　　此外，做生意回饋顧客，此乃理所當然之事。所謂有捨就有得，這也是因時制宜，來提高業績的方式之一。為了表示對客戶的重視，每年三大節日我都會用路特公司的名義送禮。禮物的價格是依據每季出貨的金額來決定的。此外，所送的禮品內容也要經過仔細研究，絕不能抱著有送就好，只是敷衍一下的心態。反而要很細心的思考，要送什麼禮能給主顧感到高興、滿意又實惠，這才能表現送禮的美意和效果。否則，若一不留神，往往會適得其反。

Besides, it was reasonable to give feedback to customers. To give is to get. I also used the methods appropriately to increase my business achievements. In order to show my respect to the customers, I would send gifts to every customer in the name of the company. The value of the gifts depended on the price of the products each season. Moreover, the gifts had to be picked carefully. We cannot be muddle on this but to think considerately. Considering what do give to make the customers happy and satisfied was the purpose of sending gifts. Otherwise we could get the opposite results.

例如：主顧比較疼老婆，就買頂級化妝品禮盒，主顧收到禮物轉給老婆，能增加他們的情感，對路特公司的印象就有加分的效果。如果有小孩和孫子，可增加頂級餅乾、巧克力。煙、酒要送給特定對象。還有主顧公司的職員，其中對採購遙控器有影響力的人員，我也另外再送禮給他們，但儘量不讓老闆本人知道。

For example, for those who love their wives, I would buy makeup gift boxes. This not only increased their relationship, but also scored for my company. For those who have children or grandchildren, I would buy fancy cookies or chocolates. Cigarettes and wines were for particular people. I also send special gifts to the customers' employees and those who had big influence in buying my remote controls. However, I did this without noticing their boss.

這種送禮方式，有意想不到的好處。產品製造過程，有時候難免會有瑕疵，如果這些職員知道了，也不會把事情擴大，因為和我的關係友善，會直接先要求我們改善，這可以避免老闆對我

的產品有不好印象。

The idea of sending gifts had an unexpected advantage. There would be some mistakes during process of producing. The staff would not talk about it even if they knew it. Due to having good relationship with me, they would just tell me to improve in person. This could avoid the boss to have bad impressions on my products.

當時全省總共有四家遙控器的廠商，我最慢出道，排行第五家。他們技術比我好，經驗又豐富，已經有固定客戶群，也因此都賺到錢了。現在他們賣遙控器比較會有選擇性：利潤要高，服務要少。我能做到的客人只有小型公司，利潤較低，又是偏遠地區。我心想，沒關係，這是好機會，只要我勤奮的做，售後服務態度又好又迅速，一定可以打開屬於我的市場。

There were four remote control factories in Taiwan. I came out late to be the fifth factory. They had better professional skills than I do, and they were all experienced with stable customer groups. Thus they had earned a lot of money. Now they had got choices selling the remote controls: high profit with low service. My customers were from small companies with low profit and located in remote districts. I thought to myself, "that's ok, no worries. This is a great opportunity. I could open my own market if I worked hard with nice attitude and good after-sale service".

做人或做生意都要講「信用」，我對信用有新的解釋：即相信自己能夠做好的事情，然後讓他人便利使用。守信用是常識，信用問題就是生存問題，尤其信用是經商之本，商人要想讓自己的事業有更長遠的發展，必須講究商業道德。如果失信於顧客，會斷送自己的前途。一個人只要真誠地待人處事，就會很容易獲得他人的好感，並且能夠得到客人的信任，客人就會選擇你所推薦的產品。

We have to be honest when getting alone with people and doing business. I have my new definition to the word "trust":

believe in yourself to do the best and benefit others. Keeping promise is a common sense. Credit problem is living problem. Especially credit is the basis of doing business. Businesspersons have to value the business morality to develop their business long-term. If you lost your credit to the customers, you would ruin your future. One has to be nice to people and work hard to be welcome by others. Also, he or she could gain the trust of customers. In other words, they would choose your products.

　我非常注重產品的品質，好的品質，就是生意賺錢的根源，因此對檢測產品要求很高，但因為我才學沒多久，所以檢測比較費時間。經過幾個月的磨練，對電子多少也有一些概念。一年之後，每個月我可以賺到自己的薪水了，雖然只是幾萬元，我已經感受到甜美的果實，讓我越來越有信心去做。

　I valued the quality of my products. The good quality is the essential elements to making money. Therefore I had high standard on testing the products. Since I was new to the business, it was time consuming for me to test the products. After a few months of learning and experimenting, I had some basic knowledge of electronics. One year later, I could earn my own salary every month. Though it was only a few ten thousand dollars, I had felt the sweetness of gaining. I felt more confident doing the business.

「真誠待客品質高，遵守諾言服務好。」
"if I will be honest to customers it is high quality that I received;
if I keep my word then I received the good reputation"

穩定成長先付出
One must pay efforts to grow steadily

　　俗語有云：「少壯不努力、老大徒傷悲。」，為免將來年老才後悔，現在的我每天都早出晚歸，一直覺得時間都不夠用。我除了要關心同仁、品質抽檢、管理進出貨、核對收支進出帳款等例行公事外，主顧來電還要和他寒暄，甚至外縣市的遙控器訂單，出貨都由我親自送到貨運行，更不用說，在台北縣市的訂單要親自送貨。

There is a proverb goes, "if one does not exert oneself in youth, one will regret it in old age". In order not to regret in my old age, I went to work early and went back home late. There is always not enough time. I had to routinely care about my staff, quality check, manage the import and export, and verify the accounting records. Moreover, I needed to answer all customers' call, and send out remote control orders to other cities; and needless to say, the orders from Taipei city and county.

　　我當時的原則是：只要有錢賺，半夜敲門叫我起床都很高興。那幾家同行都有好幾位業務人員，又懂技術，我卻是一人公司，只僱一位工讀生，現在的我只有再往前衝啦！實事求是去打這一場硬戰。雖然公司多了一個人，可是他只能幫我接電話，所有的事還是自己要去處理。回到公司要檢測廠商送來的遙控器是否正常，然後貼紙、包裝，只要人在公司就有做不完的工作。

My rule was: happy to be awake in the middle of the night as long as I am making money. Those who work in the same fields had many professional workers, but I was the only one in my own company with one part-time worker. What I could do now was to work hard and did what was right for this battle. Although I had a part-time worker, he could only pick up some phone calls for me. I had to do all the works. When I was in my company, I had to check and test the remote controls delivered from the factory to see if they functioned well, then I sticker them and packed them. I had work that could never be done.

這樣的忙碌，有時候只能買麵包或粽子在車上吃，一邊吃麵包或粽子，一邊開車，這樣能節省很多時間。每個月一定要全省跑一趟，去拜訪一次主顧。我都選擇星期六下班出發到中南部（當時公營機關星期六還要上班），隔天星期日安排拜訪主顧，夜晚回台北準備隔天上班。

A busy businessman like me only would have some bread or rice bun while I was driving to work. It would save a lot of time while I ate and drive at the same time. I needed to go all around the country to visit my customers. I would choose Saturday after work to head to the south (non-profit-organizations needed to work on Saturdays). Sundays were planned for visiting customers, and I would head back to Taipei on Sunday night for work on next day.

台北縣市利用星期一至五的晚上拜訪主顧，每天幾乎從早上忙到半夜，做每一件事都要用最快的速度去處理，能夠早點完成，就能再接下一個工作。時時提醒自己要更勤快的跑業務，也時時警惕自己的健康。因為有充沛的體力，才能走更長遠的路。

I visited customers in Taipei city and Taipei county at night after work from Monday to Friday. I was busy from early morning to midnight. I did things quickly and efficiently hoping to finish one thing so that I could do the next. I kept reminding myself to be an efficient businessman and not to ignore my health. To walk a further road, I need a better health.

　　以公司目前的業績而言，我當然有能力可以僱用一位副手。但為什麼我不僱用一位副手呢？為什麼要讓自己這樣辛苦呢？其中的原因，是因為我注意到同行所僱用的業務員，一旦這些業務員建立了自己的客源之後，往往都另起爐灶，再與自己的老東家競爭生意。這讓我警覺到這個行業請業務員是危險的抉擇，主顧很快會被搶走。所以再怎麼辛苦，還是要自己去做，才能保住自己現有的客源，而且又可以省掉一個人的薪資開銷。

　　According to the business achievement, I had the ability to hire an assistant. But why would I not hire one? And why should I work so hard? I had noticed that the other business companies from the same field hired some employees. Once the employees had their own customers, they would build up their own companies. After that, they competed with their former employers. This phenomenon reminded me the danger of hiring a worker in the business. Thus I had to work hard on my own, no matter how tired and tough, to be sure my customers would not run off. In addition, I could save money from not hiring another worker.

　　就這樣持續穩定經營，公司業績每個月都在增加。如今，台灣鐵捲門有安裝遙控器的商家達到百分之九十以上，這個成果完全是路特公司創造出來的。就是因為路特做多功能防盜鐵捲門遙控器，今天的使用率才有這麼高。倘若只是用在車庫鐵捲門，現在使用率恐怕不到百分之一的量。我到過香港，看他們使用鐵捲門的防盜方法，是在左右兩邊都上鎖。

　　The business achievement had increased every month steadily. Today, ninety percent of the stores had set up remote controls for their rolling shutters. This had to do with "Root". The success of high using rate owed to the production of Root's burglarproof rolling shutter remote control. However, the utility rate of the rolling shutter for garages had not reach one percent. I had been to Hong Kong. They had locked both sides with iron lockers on the rolling shutters.

　　香港人使用遙控器只安裝在車庫鐵捲門，因此量很少。香港有幾位客戶也經銷路特遙控器很多年了，每次當我問他們，為什麼沒辦法推展給店舖？為什麼不教育他們，路特遙控器有多功能又可防盜？他們的回答都一樣「店家已經習慣上鎖」，猶如台灣店家都安裝遙控器的習慣一樣，因為香港的店家習慣左右兩邊上鎖，要改變他們使用遙控器的習慣，可能要費許多精神和時間。

　　In Hong Kong, they only use remote controls on the rolling shutters of their garages. Therefore, the usage was really low. I had some customers from Hong Kong who sold Root's remote controls for years. Every time when I asked them why not sold the products to those stores? Why not advertise to them that Root's remote controls had a multi-function of burglarproof? They always replied with the same answer, "The stores had already got used to the locks". As if the stores were getting used to the remote controls in Taiwan. It might take time and efforts to persuade the stores in Hong Kong to use remote controls.

「少壯勤勞行苦心，駿馬奔騰報佳音。」
"When I was young I am diligence for working;
it will receive the good news"

成長、茁壯、升級
Growing, prospering, and upgrading

　　我相信慢工出細活，終有一天磨杵能成針。當時我對安裝技術、遙控功能、電子的認識，比一開始接觸時，已經了解很多，這對產品的推展有很大的幫助。第二年每個月利潤已達到十萬元，有能力僱一位電子作業員。這可以減輕我的工作量，也能讓我有更多的時間去推展業務。

I believe soft fire makes sweet malt. One day the iron bar could grind to a fine needle. I was more familiar with the remote control set up skills, remote control functions, and electronics knowledge. This is a big advance to develop our products. The profit had reached one hundred thousand the second year, and I could afford an electronic worker. This could decrease my workload, and I would have more time for developing my business.

　　第三年每月利潤達到二十萬，即使請二個員工也負荷不了當時的需求量，因此再僱一位電子作業員。就這樣，一步一腳印，我對產品的要求以及迅速貼心的服務，受到客人的讚賞，使用路特品牌遙控器的人都說好。到了第四年利潤達到三十萬，工作量當然又不能負荷，又再僱一位電子作業員。雖然生意越來越好，我也不敢掉以輕心，一點都不鬆懈。對產品的品質，還有對客人的服務態度，都未曾掉以輕心。深怕一個不小心，多年來努力的成果，就會化為烏有。

The profit reached two hundred thousand dollars during the third year that two workers could not handle the needs. Thus I hired another electronic worker. My business grew steadily, and customers complimented on my products' quality, my services and efficiency. No one complained about using Root's remote control.

During the fourth year, the profit reached four hundred thousand dollars. I hired another worker to balance the needs. Although my business had gone well, I dare not to relax. I worked harder to ensure the quality of my products and customer services; for fear that I would fail the hard work for years.

邁進第五年，每個月增加的營業額，必須再僱兩位職員，才能分擔公司的工作量，一位是會計、一位是作業員。現在如果沒有會計幫我作帳，我會忙不過來。當時每月營業額已經超過百萬，產品必須再開發新的功能，在外觀上也必須更加精緻。否則，若一成不變，很快的就會被其他同行所取代。因為產品的改良、升級，已是勢在必行的重要大事了。

In the fifth year, the turnover for each month forced me to hire another two workers. One was the accountant and one was another worker. If it was not the accountant, my business could not go so well. The profit had reached over million and the products needed to develop some new functions to attract more customers. Moreover, the design of products had to be more delicate or products from other companies would replace mine. Renewing and upgrading of products was an essential issue.

在科技日新月異的時代，我體悟到產品若不升級就會被淘汰。我今天能在市場占一席之地，所憑藉的就是掌握先機，在別人還沒看到前，我就已經投入開發了。同樣的道理，在生活水準不斷提升的年代裡，即使產品已經是市場中的主流商品，若不持續改良升級，遲早有一天會被其他更先進的產品所取代，而在市場上失去與其他產品的競爭力。

In the generation of technology highly renewing, I noticed that the products would be eliminated without keep upgrading them. The reason why I could have a market of my own today is that I grasp the chances before others do and tried hard to develop. In

other words, in the generation of high living standard, even if the products were the market trends, they would still have the chance of being replaced by other updated products. Thus, they would lose the chance to compete with other products in the market.

　我會想要將產品升級，是有一位主顧，給我的一個建議。他有一個客人是開銀樓的，建議遙控器的功能，能否再多樣化？所以我的主顧就把客戶所需的產品訊息轉達給我，讓我有了新的想法，如何去提升產品的功能性。按當時鐵捲門遙控器的功能，只有上升、下降、停止三個動作，押扣（發射器只是單鍵）以循環式控制鐵捲門。當時我做的遙控器，一般只使用在車庫的鐵捲門，以方便駕駛坐在車上手按遙控器，就能打開車庫門，而不用下車去啟動開關。在當時使用遙控器開門相當威風，是一種社會地位的表徵，會讓鄰居刮目相看。

One of the customers gave me a suggestion of upgrading and renewing the products. He had a guest who owned a jewelry store suggested that the remote control could be more multi-functional. Thus my customer told me the message of the customer's need. I suddenly had a new though toward promoting the function of the product. The original function of the remote control was "up", "down", and "pause". The buckle (the radio transmitter was only a button) controlled the rolling shutter in a circular way. My remote control was generally for garage gates that drivers could open the gates without going down their cars by using the remote control. This was a cool technique. That was also a symbol of social status that your neighbors would respect and admire you.

　當時鐵捲門遙控器算是高科技，因此價位非常高，家中有汽車，又有車庫的人才會買來用。還有特殊行業，例如銀樓或會在倉庫放貴重東西的業者。因為店家害怕固定在牆壁上，控制鐵捲門那個不銹鋼盒子裡面押扣開關被撬開，鐵捲門就會被打開而遭小偷。因此拿掉牆壁上的押扣開關，而換成安裝鐵捲門遙控器來控制上升、下降、停止，這確實有比以前安全。

The remote control was a high tech at that time so the price was relatively high. People who bought the remote control were the ones who had cars in their garages. In addition, some particular occupations would make a purchase like the jewelry stores or those who stock expensive things in their garages. The store owners were afraid that thieves would broke the stainless steel box to break the switch, so they had replaced the switch with the remote control to open and close the gate. This was definitely safer than before.

而建議我的那位店家很聰明，他認為：如果能以遙控器，去控制鐵捲門馬達的總電源，在安全上就更加有保障了。遙控器分二個步驟，先按遙控器關下鐵門，然後再按遙控器關掉馬達總電源，這樣鐵捲門絕對開不了。確實如此，用遙控器關掉鐵捲門馬達電源，真的無法再啟動鐵捲門，除非再用原來的遙控器打開，這可達到防盜功效，萬無一失。

The store-owner who gave suggestion to me was very smart. He thought it would be safer if the remote control could also control the main power source of the gate motor. The remote control had two sections: first you push the remote control to close the rolling shutter, and then you closed the main power source of the gate motor to make sure the gate would not open again. Indeed, the main power source could not be back on after turning it off. This could reach the function of burglarproof unless you open the main power again with the same button.

像這種控制方式，發射器最少需要四個獨立按鍵才能做到這樣的功能，這又比原先的科技設計更高級。但我並不畏難，聽到這個建議反而使我非常興奮。當時鐵捲門遙控器市場根本沒有公司生產這種多功能的遙控器。時勢運轉，我正想要開發新的功能，他就給我一個很好的主意。做生意都要隨時注意客人的建議

和抱怨，才會成長，決不可閉門造車，不然就是死路一條。

Imagine this kind of remote control would originally need four individual buttons to function. This was a higher level of technique. I did not afraid of difficulties and became excited when hearing suggestions. The other companies from the same field did not produce such multi-functional remote controls. The luck came as a blessing. I had a new suggestion just when I wanted to develop a new function. We had to keep customers' suggestions and complaint in mind for development when doing business. We could not build a cart behind closed doors or we would block our own paths.

「意堅勤奮超人群，技術精進時創新。」
"The strong determination and industrious than others;
the technology is progressive and innovative"

開發新產品

Developing new products

　　我非常積極的尋找更先進的開發技術人員。經過這幾年的磨練，雖然我不會開發技術，但是知道如何要求技術人員，並能針對現在消費者的需求方向而進行設計。新產品的特色，主要為：體積要小又要美觀，遙控距離要遠，且避免受干擾。上、下、停、斷電、啟動五個按鍵分開，各自單獨一個按鍵。

I was actively finding a technique worker with new skills. After a few years of experiencing and training, even though I did not understand developing skills, I knew what I want from a technician. Also, I could design directly along the customers' needs. The new products shaped smaller and had modern appearances; moreover, the remote control had to work in a distance without any interference. Open, close, pause, power off, and power on, five separated buttons had their own functions.

　　以前遙控器的功能已經不符合現在市場的需求了。這次開發擬定的方針，除了降低產品成本外，更重要的是，功能要增多，外觀要精緻好看。以這種方向來設計，產品在市場才有競爭力。因此，開發人員的技術要更高明，自然而然的開發費用也會相對提高。

The former version of the remote control had already out of fashion and did not meet market needs. The ultimate goal for this development was not only lower the cost, but more importantly, increase the function and design. Only this kind of design could compete in the market. Therefore, developers had to have higher skills, and their salary would be relatively higher.

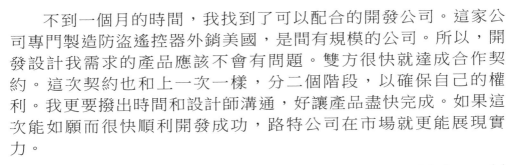

　　不到一個月的時間，我找到了可以配合的開發公司。這家公司專門製造防盜遙控器外銷美國，是間有規模的公司。所以，開發設計我需求的產品應該不會有問題。雙方很快就達成合作契約。這次契約也和上一次一樣，分二個階段，以確保自己的權利。我更要撥出時間和設計師溝通，好讓產品盡快完成。如果這次能如願而很快順利開發成功，路特公司在市場就更能展現實力。

Not until a month that I found a company which could cooperate in the development. This extensive company focused on producing burglarproof remote controls exporting to America. Thus it would not be a problem for them to design my products. The two of us had come to an agreement soon. The contract had two sections to protect my rights, just like the last one. I had to spare some time to meet the designer so the products could be produced soon. Root would be the spotlight in the market if this contract had developed successfully.

　　設計師與我集思廣益，全力以赴，在短短三個月就開發完成，需要的功能都測試成功。新研發出的產品在市面上，功能最先進，外觀最美觀，價格又低廉，真讓同行刮目相看，又提高我的營業總額。經由此次的經驗，更讓我體悟到「多聽多聞」這句話的意涵。唯有不斷接受新知、新資訊，方能不斷的進步。這次產品的升級，就是因為如此，才能佔得先機。

The designers and I were brainstorming and working, trying to develop successfully in three months and had passed the tests. The new products for sale had to have the newest function, stylish appearance, and the lowest price to earn the respects from the other companies. This could increase my business turnover. This experience taught me to "listen and learn". Only absorbing new knowledge and information could we keep progressing. Due to all that, I could have the success in upgrading and elevating my products.

　　做生意得搶先機才能迅速得利，直到今天我還是很感謝這兩位主顧。自從離鄉背井到台北，我就多聽多聞人家的建言，再經過自己的思考，認為是好的就儲存在頭腦，需要的時候拿出來應用。聽到認為不適合的就先擺在旁邊，但是也要表現感恩，絕不可駁斥對方。

We have to grasp the chance to gain in a short time when doing business. I am still thankful to these two customers today. Since I left my hometown to Taipei, I listened to the giving suggestions, think again, and save the ones that I considered the best then use it when it is needed. I would up it aside when I heard some unsuitable suggestions, but I had to be thankful as well without refuting others.

　　當新產品一推出，更要注意客人的反應、建議和抱怨。有一次有位新客人來電告知，遙控器發生問題，隔天我就親自開車到中部客人工廠了解。結果是遙控器外殼螺絲轉太緊而一直在發射，因此干擾到他家的鐵捲門遙控器，造成感應遲鈍不好用，遙控距離又縮短。

The customers' reaction toward the products, their suggestions, and complaints were the important factors when a new product launched. Once a new customer called for remote control problems, I drove down south to the customers' factory for understanding the situation. The problem was the screw on its case went too tight so the sensor kept functioning. Thus the sensor interfered with the gate remote control that blocked the function of the remote and shortened the control distance.

　　我很迅速在現場就解決了這個問題，客人感受到買我的遙控器有保障，服務態度好又迅速。讓客人很快又下一張大訂單，這次我親自開車送產品南下，一天來回。這趟利潤有二十幾萬元之多，錢賺到了，又能改善自己的產品，累積不少心得。做生意不要怕辛苦，服務要迅速，對客人要恭敬，有時候賺錢就這麼容易。不出幾個月，營業額竟然超出我意料之外，一個月總營業額達到二百萬。

I efficiently solved the problem at once that the customer felt certain that my products came with great customer service. This made the customer requested for a big order. I also drove south to deliver the orders myself. The order made two hundred dollars profit. I could improve my products with this money and I felt confident. It was easy to do business and earn money as long as you had a good customer service and respect your customers. Within a few months, the turnover was, unexpectedly, two million dollars a month.

「集思廣益心生智，辛勞自有上天助。」
"When collecting opinions of wide benefits my wisdom will be appeared; when diligence the God will help us"

生命共同體─照顧一起奮鬥的好伙伴

A life community - taking care of the fellows who worked together

　　回想來台北的第一份工作，初出茅廬、膽顫心驚。老闆對我說：「你要努力工作，否則隨時請你回家吃自己（免職）。」我心裡很害怕被解雇，因此全力以赴，認真又細心地，把我每天必需做的清潔工作做的很好，讓老闆高興是我的目標。

Recalling my first job in Taipei, I was so nervous. My boss said to me, "you have to work hard or else you will be fired." I was so afraid of being unemployed, so I worked hard on my cleaning job. My goal was to please my boss.

　　今天我有機會當一個小老闆，老天對我已經很好了，所以我應該要更努力去做好。照顧同仁是最需要去關心的事，沒有大家用心共同去創造，是不可能成功的。我了解這個道理，所以更要關愛所有的同仁。

I am lucky that I had the opportunity to be a small boss, so I had to try harder on everything. Taking care of my staffs was the priority. We would be far from success if we were not together in one mind. I care about all my staffs because I understood this concept.

　　雖然生意進展的很順利，但是我未曾鬆懈，卻更積極思考公司營業的每一件事。例如：員工的薪水、福利以及上班時間一定要重新檢討，要受到較好的待遇，要有捨才有得的觀念。

Although I had a great business achievement, I did not have time to relax. I tried hard on every little detail in my company, such as my employees' salary, their welfare benefits, and their

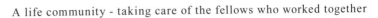

working hours. I treat my employees nicely and generously, a loss may turn out to be a gain.

　　同仁為我工作，我有照顧、關心他們的責任，我要每位同仁和我一起工作，猶如做自己的事業。上班時間感到疲倦可以自己休息，解除疲勞再做。今天精神或心情不好做少一點，等明天自己補回來。不約束、不限制，自然而然大家都非常盡職。

The staff worked for me, I care about their responsibilities. I wanted every staff who worked for me to work as if they were doing their own business. They could take a rest on duty if they felt tired, and got back to work after they felt fine. They could make up their workload the next day, if they had fallen behind a bit on work today. I do not restrain, or limit anything at work. I wanted them to be free and responsible on their own.

　　我要的是效率而不是工作時間，我不隨便看著同仁做事，工作由自己發揮，因此要大家放鬆心情工作，目的是要自己管自己。雖然公司當時同仁有十位以上，並沒有採用主管制度，我認為自己管理自己的方式會讓人更有向心力。

What I wanted was efficiency, not long working hours. I did not watch how my employees worked. A good employee should manage his or her time, so that the employees could work with a good mood and managed themselves. Even though I had over ten staffs, I did not set up a boss and employees system. I thought one would be more motivated to work for oneself.

　　十幾年來獨自一人做起不懂的生意，猶如愚公移山。製造需要很高技術的陌生產品，真是非常艱苦又耗精神。我每天都給自己很大的壓力，如果沒有堅定的精神和毅力，要成功根本就是異想天開。

I worked on my own in an unfamiliar business field over ten years, manufacturing many high-tech products that I was unfamiliar with. It was very frustrated and time-consuming. I gave a lot of pressure to myself. Without a firm mind and patience, it was impossible to success.

　　此外，管理層面最重要的就是要「將心比心」。所謂企業管理我又不懂，但要如何管理才是正確，是做生意的關鍵。我童年就踏入社會，今天有一點成就也都是向長輩學習而得來的，我的心得就是：做事要先想到他人的方便和利益，然後回頭再想自己的方便和利益。

　　Besides, the most important thing about management is to stand in others' shoes. I knew nothing about business management, but how to manage was the essential part. I worked in the society when I was young. What I had today were all learned from the elders. No matter what you do, you have to stand in others' shoes first, then turn back to think about yourself. This is what I have learned.

　　既然如此，就要先把自己的誠懇、善意、真心釋放出來，用這種方式做事比較會有圓滿結果。例如：公司一開始僱人上班共事，我就給了善意，每天上班七個小時，其他福利、薪水盡量為同仁著想。這幾年生意好、利潤多，所以每年都招待員工出國旅遊，大家都玩得非常高興。我先考慮到他們的利益，雖然一時好像是吃虧，其實對公司也有好處。

　　Thus, we have to reveal our sincere, our kindness, and our true heart. You would be closer to success if you do things with these attitudes. For example, I showed my kindness when hiring an employee. I gave him business welfare and salary for working seven hours a day. My business was successful these years with high profits so I treated my employees to go on vacations overseas every year. Everyone had great times. I would first consider their rights. Though sometimes it would be a disadvantage for me, but it turned out to benefit our company after all.

　　同仁他們都知道一般公司上班八個小時，唯有他們每天只要七個小時，如果工作超過半個鐘頭，就會付加班費。公司開始就對他們友善，所以他們也不會辜負公司，一定會有很好的表現。如此一來大家都很認真又用心的工作，我不用花時間去注意他們工作的情形，可以節省好多時間又放心去做其他事情。

The employees knew that they only had to work seven hours a day, one hour less compared with other companies. If my employees worked overtime for over half an hour, I would pay them extras. They would not fail or disappoint our company since I was kind to them from the beginning. They would have good achievements. In this case, everyone worked so hard that I did not have to spend time on checking their working condition. It would save a lot of time for me to do other businesses.

我的時間非常有限，一個人要做很多的事－送貨、收款、拜訪、維修全部自己包辦，因此時間對我來說很重要，只要公司的工作結束，就勤快地利用多餘的時間去開發客戶。同仁作業難免會有差錯，有了差錯我不會責怪他們或生氣，而會用溫和的語氣向他們解說錯的原因，然後請他們改善，他們也都欣然的接受，並且會做得更完善。好幾個職員都做了二十年。員工任職越久，累積的經驗越多，對公司越有利。如果公司經常換職員，公司就會有損失，這是非常重要的管理策略。

My time was limited that I had to deliver, collect the payments, visit, and repair. I did all these on my own; therefore time was very important to me. As long as I got off at work, I would use my spare time to survey more clients. It was an unavoidable problem that employees might make mistakes. I would not blame them or got mad, but kindly explained to them about the mistakes. After I asked them to improve, they would accept the advice and would do better the next time. Many of them had been my employees for over twenty years. The longer the employees stay the more experience they would get. That would benefit the company. It was a loss to the company if they often replaced their employees. This is an important manage strategy.

「團結一致共有心，誠心待人生意興。」
"When we have the intent of working, when we treat anybody with sincerity our business will be prosperous"

先苦後甘

No pain, no gain

　　「萬丈高樓平地起」，凡事只要根基穩固，一定會成功的。
經過這些年的努力，每月營業額將近四百萬了，才感受到賺錢很
容易。雖然覺得賺錢不是件難事，但卻也是之前付出很大的心
力，是很辛苦換來的成果。我此時心想，賺錢機會難逢，一生可
能也只有一次機會，景氣雖然好，也不可能持續很長時間，很快
就是過去式。

　　Great oaks from little acorns grow. If you worked hard and
be practical, you will definitely be successful. These years of hard
working had made my business achievement to nearly four million
dollars. Not until now that I feel how easy it was to earn money.
Although making money was not so hard, I paid a lot of efforts
to it. I earned this result. I thought to myself, that it was a rare
opportunity of making money. It was once in a lifetime experience.
Even though the economy was quite prosperous, it would not last
long.

　　生意競爭，利潤隨時在變動，所以要全力以赴，不可鬆懈。
現在辛苦一天，等到時機不好要辛苦一個月。小時候常聽到父母
親和長輩說：「先苦後甘」，到今天還是記憶猶新，真有道理。

　　The profit was always changing while the business was
competing. I had to be prepared. Now I worked hard for a day,
but I had to work so hard for a month when the bad times came.
I heard elders say "no pain, no gain", and it makes good sense
until today.

　　我自己就是活生生的見證，回想三十幾年前我購買第一棟公
寓房子，自備款七萬。當時如果拿這些錢去買一部最頂級的偉士

牌機車先享用（當時一部偉士牌機車六萬五千元），就不會有今天。購買房子和機車的抉擇改變了我一生的命運。所以說做對一件事一輩子輕鬆，這也是先苦後甘的一個例子。這棟房子到現在大約已收了五百萬元的租金了，目前市價也近千萬。賺到錢我不亂花，也不買股票，我又沒時間打牌。回憶當兵時向我問路的那位老奶奶的遭遇給我的警惕，提醒我要把錢全部存起來。

My life is a good example. I had seventy thousand for the down payment. If I bought a top Vespa (a Vespa cost sixty thousand and fifty dollars then), I would not have what I had today. The choice between buying a house or a Vespa had changed my life. If doing one thing right, you would have a whole relaxing life. This was an example of no pain, no gain. I had earned five million dollars from the rent of the house. It cost ten million dollars in the market price. I did not spend the money I earned, I did not use them for stocks, and I had no time to gamble. I remembered the advice from the old lady I met when I served the army, and I saved all the money.

有了錢也要隨時提醒自己，一定會有人來找我投資其他事業，或介紹賺錢更快的途徑，這可要注意了！我都不會動心起念，因為，我認為好賺的事業或買賣，相對賠錢也比較快，風險當然也很高，而且要小心詐騙。以前我投資不動產買賣，現在對不動產較有經驗。這幾年經營遙控器賺的錢全部購買中古屋，整修隔成雅房或套房出租。我有一個原則，租金要比鄰近便宜十分之一以上，服務也要好，和做生意一樣，因此很少會換房客，每年租金收入很穩定。

When I had saved money, I had to remind myself that people would ask me to do investment or introduced me a quicker way to earn money. I had to take notice on these and I would not be tempted. I think these easier ways of making money would lead to quicker ways of losing money. Relatively the easy ways of making money would often be risky. I used to invest real estate so I was more experienced with the business. I used the money earned from selling the remote control on buying the old second-hand houses. Then I rebuilt it or made it into apartments for rent. I had a rule that the rental must be 10 percent lower than the rent in the neighborhood. Also, I insisted in good service just like doing business. Therefore my guests seldom move and I got steady rentals.

　　不動產景氣開始回升的時候，一些朋友建議我再兼做中古屋買賣。雖然有了經驗，但是一個人的能力有限。我的理念是：人的時間、精力有限，不可以分散精力，所以我決定專心持續認真做好遙控器。一生做對一個行業已經很有福報了，所以要更用心做好產品，來回饋顧客。不可以分散精力，而導致連本行都沒做好，而損失主顧利益。今天賺到的錢都是受到顧客的恩惠，因此我要專心一致做得更好。

　　Some friends recommended that I sold old houses again as a part time job when it started to get prosperous in the real estate business. Though I was experienced, my abilities were limited. My principles are: "our time and abilities were limit, so we could not do many things at a time". I decided to focus on the business of remote- controls. It is lucky blessed to do a right business in life, so I needed to do it better as a feedback to my customers. If we do many things at a time, then we could loss some benefits and did badly on the main task. The money I made today had to do with the mercy of my customers and clients, thus I had to focus and worked harder.

「辛苦後甘如是寶，省吃儉用好到老。」
"As treasury we will have a sweetish taste after working hard; if we save money on food and expenses then we will be good until the end of life"

靈活變化，掌握先機

Be creative and grasp the opportunities

　　有志者事必成，我在這行經歷過艱苦的奮鬥，終於有了一點成果。這些年來付出很多的心血，才有今天業績上亮麗的表現。但關於遙控器市場發展的動向，還是不能掉以輕心。尤其價格方面，路特公司產品的售價，一直是市面上最高的。

　　Where there is a will, there is a way. After all the hard working in the business, I finally had some achievements and success. I paid a lot of efforts to have a good grade. However, I could not be too careless about the development of the remote control market, especially the price, because Root has the highest price in the market.

　　目前賣遙控器的人越來越多，使用遙控器已普及化。此一行業都有很多人做，相對的市場也就愈來愈競爭。所以唯有隨時貫注精神，掌握整個產業的環境變化，就好像在戰場上一樣，隨時要瞭解敵情狀況。做生意本來就是如此，沒有一個行業是例外的。社會資源是大家的，端看你如何發揮，猶如在比賽，能夠脫穎而出，成功就是你的。

　　More and more people bought remote controls, and they became popular. Many businesses had started to produce the remote control and the market became very competitive. Therefore I had to be really concentrated and focused on this variable industry, just like a war. I had to know my competitor well. This is how the business work, not other exceptions. The social resources belong to everybody, and everybody use it in different ways. It was as if you were in a game: if you are the outstanding one, the success is yours.

　　公司隨時要改變營運策略，才不會被淘汰。首先要做的是，如何降低公司產品的價格，來增加產品在市場的競爭力。因此，我思考自己建立生產線來降低成本，產品在市場才有競爭力。經過多年的磨練，自己生產對我而言已不是問題。為了生產必須培訓一位測試人員、一位電子工程師，未來市場一定會有一場大戰，有了萬全準備才能永續經營。半年之後，在我預料之中，遙控器價位好像在溜滑梯，一直往下滑，還好降價的因應措施我早就準備好了。

　　Our company had to modify our operating strategy so as not to be excluded. What we had to do first was decreasing the price of the products to raise their competiveness in the market. Hence, I considered setting up our own production line to lower the costs. After a few years of training and work experiences, production line for me was not a big deal. I had to train a testing staff, and an electronic engineer. There would be a big war in the future market so we had to be well prepared for sustainable operation. After six months, just like what I had foreseen, the price of the remote control was continuously sliding down. There is no need to worry because I had all the backup plans in mind already.

　　這幾年台灣電子業、電腦業蓬勃發展，技術進步均非常迅速，也因此製造遙控器再也不是高科技了。目前市場超過數十家遙控器廠商，新品牌都用價格來吸引客人，如果我賣的價錢不高於他牌很多，主顧還是會選用路特老品牌。如果差價太多，即使再死忠的主顧也會跑掉，不但要適當的調整價位，也要用心經營。

　　The electronic industry and the computer industry had increased prosperously. Their skills improved rapidly as well so the making of the remote control was not a high-tech anymore. There were over ten factories in the market producing remote controls, and new brands used lower prices to attract customers. The old customers would choose Root if my price was not too much higher than the other brands. If I overcharge too much, even the oldest customers would run away. We had to carefully arrange the price, and patiently operate the company.

又過了幾年，遙控市場越來越競爭，利潤也不如前幾年，我也要想辦法增加營業項目，來提高公司收入，所以我開始尋找有關遙控器的周邊配備。後來得知市場有一種產品最適合和遙控器配套銷售，雖然這種馬達用量不多，但是利潤很好。我又立即上網找到我要的產品，打電話跟國外廠商洽談之後，很快就進口樣品。經過測試沒問題，就先訂一批進來銷售，這就多一項營業項目，可增加收入，每年更多了不少利潤，有時候賺錢就是這麼容易。

After few years, the remote control market had become more and more competitive, and the profit was not as good. I had to think of a way to increase my business categories and raise the company income. Thus I started to search for the accessories of remote controls. I realized there was a product in the market that suited our product very well. Though there were not a lot of these kinds of motors in the market, they would bring good profits. I immediately search for the products I wanted and import some samples after calling the company abroad for arrangements. After there was no problem with the samples, I called for more orders of the product. Then I got an extra business category for more income and gain more profit every year. Making money is just so easy.

「貫注精神上戰場，用心經營續發揚。」
"We concentrate spirit on battlefield; we promote
diligently on business in a sustainable development"

泰山之巔，豈一蹴可幾？

Rome was not build in a day

　　我作夢也想不到有今天的成就，雖然不是很富有，但是我已經很滿足現在所擁有的一切。我一生的命運過程，猶如遠洋巨輪衝破驚濤駭浪，昂然駛向前方。

It was like a dream to have the achievement today. Though I was not very rich, I was satisfied with everything I had now. The fate of my life was like a huge ship ran into a giant wave and head straight fearlessly.

　　回顧十幾年前束手無策，動魄驚心的躺在台大醫院急診室，絕望、驚險又無奈的心境和現在比較猶如在作夢。我想這是命運的安排吧！昔日同事和朋友知道我做遙控器又做得有聲有色，大家都跌破眼鏡。如果我是做自由業或其他不是電子相關產業的行業，他們還比較不感到驚訝。他們都說：「絕！」。

Remembering the clueless situation ten years ago, I laid desperately in the emergency bed of National Taiwan University hospital. Compared to the situation now, it was like a dream. I think this is my fate. My former colleagues and friends could not believe their ears when hearing that I was in the business of remote control and it was a big success. If I were a free lancer or were not in the electronic industry, they would not be so surprised. They said, "Superb!"

　　一個完全不懂的行業，又自己一個人獨撐大局，做到全台灣省銷售第一名，可想而知，我花了多少心血，真的使我耗盡精力。有時候也很佩服自己一個人有這麼大的能耐。以前那四家做遙控器前輩同行，目前也都轉業了，有的開計程車，還有開麵食泰山之巔，豈一蹴可幾？
Rome was not build in a day

105

店。

    With a business that I was totally unfamiliar with and I ran all the errands all by myself, it was obvious how much efforts I paid to be the top one all over Taiwan. Sometimes I was amazed by myself to have such ability. The other four companies in the same field manufacturing remote controls transferred their careers. Some worked as a taxi driver and some opened a noodle stand.

    可想而知，鐵捲門遙控器這行真的很難做。可喜的是，我現在還能保持最多的銷售量。全台灣鐵捲門工廠幾乎都知道路特這個品牌，大部份也都在使用路特遙控器，但是我還是要全力以赴。

    It was obvious that the remote control for the iron rolling gate was a tough business. I was glad that my market share was still on the highest. Almost all of the iron rolling gate factories in Taiwan know this brand "Root". They were mostly using Root's remote controls, yet I still need to work hard.

「鴻皓之志憑本事，無心插柳終有成。」
"The far-reaching ambition is a ability; unintentional actions may bring unexpected success"

成功經營面面觀

The aspects of success

　　多元化的社會，任何行業都有很多人在經營。做生意的人，都想要在最短的時間內賺很多錢。雖然，每個人經營的理念都不一樣，但是一般人都認為，只有認真、辛苦的經營，才能賺到錢。然而在現實生活中，其實並不盡然。

　　In a multi-cultural society, any business is very competitive. People doing business wanted to make money with the least efforts. Although the idea of running a company differs with everyone, everyone thinks that the only way of making money is to work hard. However, I was totally different in real life.

　　做生意宛如一場比賽，自己認為有實力才會參加比賽。對一位經營者而言，資金就是選手、認真的態度就是選手的體能、經營者的聰明才智就好比選手的技術一般，三者缺一不可。參賽者的實力都很強，能夠在強勁的對手中脫穎而出，最後得到勝利，絕非偶然僥倖的。做生意和比賽一樣，競爭很激烈，是完全憑實力來定勝負的。

　　Doing business was like attending a competition. We only sign up for the competition if we think we were skilled and had the ability to do so. For a business operator, the fund is the contestant, the hard working attitude is the strength of the contestant, and operator's wisdom and ideas were like the skills of the contestant. The three were equally important. The contestants got good abilities and the one who stood out from other competitors got the trophy.

常有人問我，你做這行似乎沒什麼競爭對手，是不是比較好做？其實隔行如隔山，沒做過的人是不會理解的。在多元化的社會，我還沒找到哪一行不競爭的，大家都拼得非常兇猛，就像棒球比賽一樣，一不小心就被三振出局。

People often asked me whether it was an easy job while I got few competitors. In fact a change of profession often means a different field of knowledge. People would not understand without trying and experiencing themselves. I did not know any profession which was not competitive. In today's society, everyone competes fiercely, just like a baseball game. You are out after accidentally three strikes.

做生意就是想要賺錢，最不想遇到客人殺價而吃虧。可是客戶反應價錢也是好事，更能了解市場的需求價格，給客人滿意的價格，就會減少客戶的流失率。客人都有貨比三家不吃虧的心態，所以對價格一定要能瞭若指掌。

We do business to make money, and the least thing we wanted to encounter was that we had taken advantage. It was a good thing that customers reject our price; it would help us to caught attention of the reasonable market price. We gave good prices to our customers to decrease the lost of our customers. The customers would compare between prices in order to get a good deal, so we must know the market price well.

做生意要隨時注意市場動向，隨時要有危機意識，以及善後的準備和對策。如果客人反應產品價格、品質、服務，這可要好好的反省，不要只認為自己的品質好、價錢公道。做生意唯一的觀念是：如果同樣的產品，同行可以賣這個價格，我的產品同樣價錢，一定也可以賣，否則就是採購和管理有缺失，需要重新檢討、追根究底。客人的建議不可以當作耳邊風，不然很快就關門大吉了。

We had to focus on market trends, have consciousness on crisis when doing business, and prepare a plan for any situations. We also had to reflect ourselves if the customers had problems on the product price, quality, or service. Do not be too proud about our good quality and good price. One important concept on business is that we could have the same price as other companies did, or else our company failed on purchasing and managing. Then we would need to reflect ourselves on the problems. Customers' suggestions were very important for us, and we need to keep them in mind in order to keep the business going.

　　很多人做生意，到最後都是失敗者居多，其實有很多原因。有的人做生意很認真，可是方法不對，沒用心。無論做哪一種行業，都要認真、用心、細心、多聞、多問、誠懇待人，甚至非常小的細節都要用心去思考，否則想要賺到錢，無異於緣木求魚。

Many businesses ended up unsuccessfully due to many reasons. Some worked hard without a good method, and they did not worked diligently. No matter which occupation, we must work firmly with our true hearts. We do things carefully, listen more, and be kind to others. Even the most detailed trifles should be taken care of, or else it would be impossible to make money.

　　也有的人很專心經營，可是最後還是一無所有，其親友都覺得不可思議。因為有些人剛做生意賺到錢，就毫無顧忌地過著很奢侈的生活，以為賺錢很容易，而沒意識到賺錢的好機會不可能持續很久的。而且把賺錢的黃金時間浪費掉，無心照顧生意，奢侈享受，花錢如流水，久而久之而上癮，每天都想去找樂子，這也是失敗原因之一。

Some were also working hard on their career but eventually got nothing. Their relatives and friends were surprised. That was because they spent their money living luxurious after they had made some money. They thought making money was easy but forgot that the good chance did not stay long. They often ignored their business to enjoy luxurious lives and missed the opportunities of making more money. After they had used to the happiness, their business started to fail.

其實剛做生意要更節儉，如果賺到錢存起來，資金就會寬裕。如遇上市場競爭或不景氣，有了充裕的資金，就拼得過人家了。經營事業有很多料想不到的情況發生，所以要未雨綢繆，以備不時之需。做生意就是這麼難，因此俗語說：「要生一個會做生意的人很難」，所以才有職員和僱主來扮演不同的角色，才能衍生共同合作「經營事業」，否則大家都是老闆，哪來職員。

In fact, we should be provident when starting a business. We would have plenty of money for fund if we save all we have earned. In addition, we would defeat other companies by having enough funds when the market competes or the economic falls. There were a lot of unpredictable things happened while doing business, so we had to get everything prepared beforehand just in case. This was the difficult part of doing business. A proverb goes, "it is hard to be a person who is good at doing business". Therefore there were employees and employer doing their own jobs to cooperate on a business. If everyone is the boss, then who is going to be the employees?

「奢侈花錢如流水，浪費時間永不回。」
"We spend money luxuriously as flowing water;
if time wastes it never comes back"

生命的轉折
The turning point of life

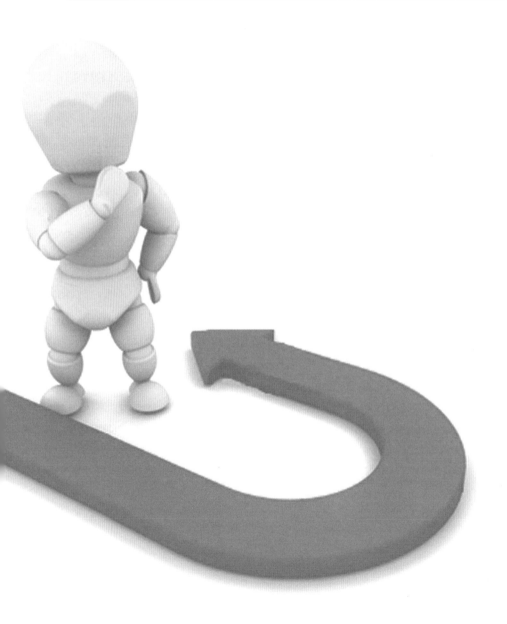

不知名的怪病
An unknown weird syndrome

　　這些年來，只關注在事業的發展，沒有把自己的身體照顧好，可能是經年累月積勞成疾，體力終究是有限的，因此身體越來越不好，甚至有時候整晚都無法入眠。到後來幾乎每個夜晚都睡不好，又沒有食慾，心跳加速，越來越沒體力，好像快撐不下去。

　　After all these years, all I cared about is the development of my career and ignored my health. It might be the years of hard working and my body had reached its limit. My health became worse and sometimes I could not sleep all night. At the end I had a hard time sleeping almost every night, and I had no appetite, heartbeat went fast, and I felt weak.

　　心想，是否舊疾復發？趕緊到住家對面的台北醫學大學附設醫院就診，並且要求住院檢查身體。這幾年來，我沒有一天能真正休息，趁著住院檢查，讓身體休息也好。而然住進醫院，每個夜晚躺在病床上，還是無法入睡。那幾天只有打點滴，因為還沒檢驗結果，因此醫生也不配藥給我吃。當時檢驗要一、二天的時間，不像現在這樣迅速，當天就會有結果。經過了幾天檢查，醫生的報告是：「全身大致正常」。

　　I thought it was the reoccurrence of my old illness. I went to the Taipei Medical University Hospital across my house for a healthy checkup. I cannot really rest during all these years. It was quite nice to stay in the hospital to check-up my health and rest. However, I still could not sleep every night in the hospital. I only had intravenous drip because the checkup result had not come out yet, and the doctor did not give any medicine to me. The checkup took one to two days, unlike today that the result would come out on the same day. After a few days of checkup, it said "generally normal" on the evaluation column.

　　十幾年前住進台大急診室，醫生是說我「無藥可治」，這次生病為什麼檢查結果卻是正常？真是令我百思不解。我住在醫院時，感覺到非常痛苦，自己知道病得很厲害。沒想到檢查結果卻是全身正常，也因此醫生沒開藥，只給我打葡萄糖點滴。可是病情不但沒改善，反而越來越嚴重，老天好像又再次開我玩笑。我要求醫生重新詳細檢驗一次，醫生也依照我的要求又做了一次抽血檢查，結果報告還是正常。

　　Ten years ago when I was in the emergency room of National Taiwan university hospital, the doctor evaluated me as "hopeless" . Why was the result "normal" this time? This confused me. I felt pain all over my body when I was in the hospital, and I knew I was seriously ill. The checkup this time was surprisingly normal so the doctor did not give me any medicine but the glucose drip. However, the sickness did not recover and it got worse and severe. It seems like God was joking again. I asked the doctor for a more detail checkup, and the doctor did do my blood check again. The result showed to be normal again.

　　老天！我已經一個星期無法入睡，怎麼檢查會正常呢？醫生要根據檢查結果，才可以配藥給病人吃，我檢查一切正常，醫生當然也不會給我藥吃。我躺在病床上，每天不能入睡，身體越來越虛弱。我再求醫生給我藥吃，醫生只說：「真的不知道要給你吃哪一種藥，因為你的檢查報告，完全沒有問題。」我就這樣痛苦的在病床上，足足躺了兩個星期。

　　Jesus, I cannot sleep for a week. How come it could be normal? The doctor had to give medicine according to the result. Yet my result showed normal so he would not give any medicine to me. I lied on the hospital bed having insomnia and felt weaker and weaker. I asked for medicine but the doctor said, "I really don't know what medicine I should give you. It showed normal on the result" . Therefore, I lay painfully on the bed for two weeks.

　　一般人三天沒睡覺就受不了，我那時已經十幾天沒辦法睡了，醫生每天給我吃的安眠藥只能淺睡約三十分鐘，兩個眼睛閉

著，很想睡，卻還是睡不著。有時候全身肌肉緊繃，心跳加速，又會盜汗。這種痛苦猶如在地獄，「生著不如死、活著很痛苦、想死又死不了、又不可自殺死。」，這種狀況，沒有經歷的人是無法體會到的。直到現在想到當時情景，還會心驚膽寒，那時的痛苦，比起上次生病，在台大急診室裡等死，還要痛苦好幾倍。

People would start to feel dizzy after three days without sleep. I had been awake for more than ten days. The sleeping pills from the doctor could only last for thirty minutes. My eyes were closed and I tried so hard to fall asleep, but I just can't. Sometimes the muscles would tightened up all over my body, and I would be sweaty because my heartbeat gone so fast. I felt like hell with all these pain. I would rather die than to live so painful like that. I could not die and I could not kill myself. One could not understand if one had no personal experience of this condition. I would still be frightened by the situation. The pain at that time was a few times serious than waiting death at the National Taiwan University Hospital.

後來醫生要我出院回家，理由是勞保規定住院期限到了，而且醫生又認為我沒病，護士說我好像是個精神不正常的人，因為全身檢查都沒事，還要住在醫院。當時我心想，這又是為什麼？面對這解不開的謎，我不知所措，最後只好心不甘情不願的辦手續出院回家。

Later on the doctor asked me to go home because the labor insurance for staying in the hospital was due. Plus, the doctor thought I was not sick or ill and the nurses thought I was crazy because I lived in the hospital with a healthy checkup result. I thought to myself, how could that be? I do not know what to do with this mystery, so I went home unwillingly.

「積勞成疾沒體力，痛苦猶如在地獄。」
"As break down from constant overwork we have
no energy; as in the hell it is very painful"

脫胎換骨悟真諦

Reborn and grasp the true essence

　　回到家依然很痛苦，當天下午我和家人商量去掛腦神經門診，掛好號，家人帶我到醫院去，卻發生醫生臨時請假。運氣真是壞。既然休診，人也來了，那就看精神科門診，心想反正差不多，有看病就好，才不會白走一趟。輪到我看診，進了診察室，這位醫生看起來大約七十歲，相貌慈祥，我坐在他的正前方，他問了我的症狀，我回答我整天不能睡覺，已經快撐不下去，感覺快死掉了。

　　I still was painful after getting home, so I discussed with my family that afternoon about going to a clinic for cranial nerves. After the registration, my family took me to the hospital and realized that the doctor was off duty. I really had a bad luck. Since I was there and I had registered already, I went to the neurology department. "The two departments were quite similar and I was there, so why not see a doctor", I thought. The doctor with a kind face seemed in his seventies. He asked my syndromes, and I answered that I could not sleep. I really felt like dying.

　　他說：「依我的診斷，你的病是憂鬱症，自律神經失調，平常給自己壓力太大，就會得這種病。憂鬱症利用儀器是無法檢查出來的。這種憂鬱症是這幾年才比較多，以前很少有，也因此很多住院醫生還不是很了解這種疾病。你要趕快吃藥和調整自己的壓力，放鬆自己，心要平靜，不然很快會沒命。」終於有醫生知道我的病症，我當下非常高興。有救了，終於有醫生願意開藥給我吃。

He replied, "according to my diagnosis, you had dysautonomia which lead to melancholia. You would be depressed if you pressure yourself too hard. Depression or melancholia could not be detected by machines. It was a very new syndrome. Therefore many doctors did not know too much about this new disease. You should take medicine and find a way to relax. You had to be calm or else it would destroy you." I was very happy at the moment that finally there was a doctor who could diagnose my sickness. Finally there was a doctor who was willing to prescript medicine for me.

我回家立即吃藥，很快淺睡三個小時，睡起來精神好很多。當天晚上再吃藥，又睡到凌晨四點，有了睡眠，精神和體力也隨著恢復起來。就這樣被這位慈祥醫生救我一命。直到現在還是非常感恩他，這是我一生中第三次面臨死亡，也是最痛苦的一次經驗。經過這次生病的經驗，使我的人生觀有很大的轉變。

I took the medicine as soon as I got home and had sleep for three hours and I felt much better when I got up. I took some medicine that night and woke up at four in the morning. I felt more energy with some sleep. The kind doctor saved my life. I was very thankful today for what he had done. This was the third time facing death in my life and it was the worst experience. The experience had changed my prospects toward life.

以前永遠是將做生意擺在第一位，現在開始覺得自己的身體比做生意重要，所以要好好的照顧自己的健康。但是艱辛開創的鐵捲門遙控器生意當然還是會持續經營下去。一生有一次做對行業也是宿世修來的。所以要以感恩的心去做得更完善。緊要關頭逢貴人，慈祥醫生救一命。

I put my business in the first place, but now I knew health means a lot more than business. We should take good care of our health. However, the business of the remote control would still run hard. Doing the right business in the first time of life was what I have practiced for. I would do my best and be thankful. An important person would always come out in the right time, like the kind doctor who saved my life.

經過這次起死又回生的體悟，我才真正瞭解到生命的可貴，因此對錢財的多寡、有無也比較看得開了。

Experiencing death and being brought back to life that I truly understood the value of life. I did not care much on money after all.

人的一生中，究竟有什麼價值，值得我們不斷去追求的呢？我覺得先要管理規劃自己的生命。

What is the true essence of life that we should pursue? I think we should manage and plan our own lives.

可是要如何發揮生命意義，說實在的，即使到了我這把年紀，也還不能完全了解，也沒概念。如同我剛開始學做不動產買賣、自己開發和販賣遙控器的情況一樣。所以現在準備去研究生命的價值，還有生存的意義。

How do we bring the true essence of life into full play? In fact, I still cannot understand entirely in my age now, and I had no idea how to reach it. Just like I started to do the real estate business, and I developed the business of the remote control. Thus now is the time for me to learn the true value and meaning of life.

　　這對我來說是一門很深奧精妙的學問，原因是我沒受過高等教育，識字又不多，所以不懂一些大道理。可是我回想這幾十年來，在社會上與待人處事上的經驗，從中獲得了很多生存的真理。

　　This was a profound issue to me; because I graduated from elementary school and did not understand many words, not to say the meaningful truth. However I did learn a lot true meaning of life from the experiences working in the society and getting along with people during these years.

　　因此，我就朝這方面去思考、探索。果然發現生命的意義，不只是創造自己的未來，更重要的是――要能利益他人。有捨就有得，有因就有果，亦叫做因果。如做應該去做的事，幫助真正需要幫助的人，這些都是種好因，因此人生就活得更有價值、有意義。

　　Thus, I had decided to start thinking and searching from this angle. I realized that we not only create our own meaning of life, but more importantly, to benefit others. We gave up something to gain more, and causes lead to effects. This also called "karma". Doing what we supposed to do and helped others were all good causes. These would make your life more valuable and meaningful.

「起死回生知感恩，生命意義助人群。」
"When I was brought back from dying I know the thanksgiving;
when we help others we have meanings in my life"

運轉命運—宿世的因今世的果

Changing the fate – the cause of the previous life and its effects on the present life

　　命運是宿世做過的因，今生受到的果。就如種瓜得瓜、種豆得豆，今世所遭遇到被人欺辱、陷害或自己受到種種的困苦，我們都想盡辦法要擺脫，可是事實都很難改變現況。一般人如果遭遇到困境常會怨天尤人，自己認為今生又沒做錯什麼大事，老天卻給我不公平待遇。

　　Fate is the cause of your previous life, and the effect of your present life. As we sow, so shall we reap. We would want to get rid of the situations when been humiliated, hurt by others, or even suffered from our own difficulties. However, it is impossible to change the facts. People would blame others for the difficulties they had been facing, and thought why God would treat them so unfair since they had done nothing bad.

　　其實懷疑老天也有道理，因為宿世做的事，今生當然不知道。好比受刑人被關在牢裡，他為什麼坐牢，我們不知道，可是他坐牢我們看到了，所以我們知道他一定曾經犯過錯。做錯事就必須坐牢，這就是因果。我們看不到每一件事的因，看到的總是他們的果；我們雖然不知前世種下什麼因，但是我們既然看到今世的果，就能知道前世種的因。所謂因果就是自己的命運。一般人如果不稱意或遇到難以解決之事，會想藉由改運解決。我認為「命」是要依靠自己去運轉，如果想轉好運結善果，必須要先種好因結善緣。好像重新為自己愛吃的果樹播種，有一天長大了，結出你想要的果實。這就是「運轉命運」。

　　In fact it was reasonable to doubt God. We would not know what we have done in the previous life. Just like those prisoners in jail. We do not know why they were behind bars for, but we knew

they had done something bad. People were sentenced to jail when committing crimes. This is the cause and effect. We did not see the cause of everything, yet we always see their effects. Though we did not know what cause had been plant in the previous life, the effects of the present life we see reflected the cause of the previous life. The cause and effect was the so-called fate. People would want to change their lucks whenever they had bad lucks or came into difficulties. I think everyone could change and control his/ her own fate. We needed to plant good cause for a good effect. It was just like planting a tree of your favorite fruit. One day it would grow the fruit you want. This is "changing the fate (luck)".

「命中注定」大家耳熟能詳。但是真有一個操縱命運的主宰嗎？答案是肯定的，那就是－－「自己」。人是命運的主角，卻常為命運所戲弄！要當命運的主人翁就要走出被命所「運」的陰霾，成為一個勇敢的人，不要做一個命運的奴隸，而是要當命運的主人，「運命」的勇者。只要肯努力和儘量修善、佈施、積陰德，有一天就會「運轉」福來。好比種果樹一樣，只要用心灌溉，一定能結出甜美的果實，這就是改造命運的根源啊！這是「運轉命運」。

Everybody heard of "destiny". Is there anyone who could be in charge of the fate? The answer is positive, and the person is "you". People were the main character of their own fates; however, they were often trick by their fates. To be the owner of your fate, you must walked out the fate which controlled by luck. We must be brave instead of being the slave to our own fates. We must be the owner of our fate and the brave who controlled fate. One day the fate would change and you'll be lucky if you work hard, be kind, and do good things. It was like planting a fruit tree: the fruits would be sweet if you watered it patiently. This was the basic of changing your luck.

不被命運束縛，才是命運的主人，真正掌握、操縱命運的智者。只要肯努力和盡力行善，一定可以改變自己的命運。所謂斷惡修善、災消福來，這是改造命運的基本原理啊！因果改不了，這是一般人的看法。雖然說「命」一定有，但是平常人才會被命所束縛。要是一個慈善的人，命就拘他不住了。有善心的人，儘管他的命裡注定要受苦，但他常以慈悲心待人，有行善的力量，就可以使他運轉命運；明明是貧賤、短命，最後卻能變成富貴長壽。而極惡的人，命也拘不住他。因為極惡的人，儘管他命中要享福，但是如果常常為惡，這惡果累積的力量，就能夠使福變成禍；本可享有富貴、長壽，最終則會變成短命、貧賤。所以，命的「因」是由自己所造，善、惡是「果」。造惡就惡果來，減壽、損福自不在話下。反之，修善就自然有好報。好比一個人砍掉果樹，今後就吃不到果實了。另一個人栽培果樹，結果之後可享用，這也是「運轉命運」。

　　Not being tied up by your fate, you could be the owner of your fate to truly control the fate with wisdom. We could definitely change and control our fates by working hard, being kind to others, and doing good things. Cutting out the bad things to be kind, and swiping out the bad luck to welcome the good were the basic rules of changing luck. People thought that the fate could not be changed. Thought everyone has their own fate, only the normal people would be controlled by fate. The fate could not tie a kind person up. When having a kind heart, even thought he/ her was meant to be suffer from pain and difficulties, he/ her would have a power of kindness that allowed him/ her to change their own fate. The poor, or those who die young, could eventually be rich with a long life. On the other hand, the fate could not grasp those evil and bad. Though they were meant to be enjoying the wealth and happiness, they did bad and evil things which would turn fortune into misfortune. Those who ought to enjoy and be happy could be poor and sick. Therefore, we create "the cause" of your fate, and kindness and evil are "the effect". If you do evil things, then you will have misfortune or bad luck. On the contrary, doing kind things and being kind will bring good luck and fortune. As if you cut down the fruit tree, then you could never taste the sweetness of the fruits. A person who watered and took good care of the tree could taste the fruits. These were also called "the changing of the

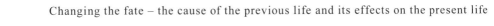

fate".

佛家講的是善惡因果報應，一定是好的有好報，做惡的必定會有苦報，決不會不報，只是時辰未到。就像影子一樣，人到哪裡，影子也在哪裡。有時候我們會懷疑，有些行善的人反而沒好運，作惡的人卻很發達。其實作惡的人以前種的果樹已結了果實，現在正在享用，如果他不再種果樹了，有一天吃完了，苦就來了。作善的人種下果樹，剛萌芽長出，要等到長大結了果實才能享受，是時間未到，而不是做善沒好處。平常人被世俗的見解所蒙蔽，這顆靈明的心塵埃尚未拂拭乾淨，不像菩薩能洞視過去、未來，而不受時空限制。所以說善、惡是果報分明的，只是一般人看不到。

The Buddhist talked about the cause and effect of kindness and evil. The kind must be treated well with fortune and the evil must receive misfortune. The bad luck would definitely come, time that matters. It was like a shadow that follows wherever we go. Sometimes we would doubt that kind people suffered from misfortune and those evil people were enjoying good fortune. In fact, the tree planted from those evil had grown fruits and they were enjoying them. If the evil would not plant again, soon the fruits will be gone and they will suffer from misfortune. The tree planted from the kind had just begun to grow and they have to wait until later for fruits. Not that they could not taste fruits, they would have to wait until the right time for fruits to grow. People had been blindfolded with social viewpoints and their hearts needed to be whipped clean. They were not like God who would not be limited by time and could know the past, present, and future. Therefore evil and kind were clearly separated. Just that not everyone sees it.

「修善仁義盡是道，運轉命運常普照。」
"When we do good, benevolence and righteousness it is overall path; when we operate our fate we illuminate all things"

方便法門—佈施

A shortcut - alms to needy

　　捐助金錢物質不是唯一的佈施方式。一般而言，佈施的方式有四種：

　　Donating money and goods were not the only way to charity. Generally, there were four ways to give alms.

　　一、金錢佈施：這是一般人都知道的，把金錢或物資分享給真正需要幫助的人，這叫做佈施。佈施財物，不是以量來衡量功德。假如有一千萬財產的人，佈施一萬元，和另一個人的財產只有一萬元，而他佈施十塊錢，兩個人比較起來，佈施十塊錢的人比佈施一萬元的還要多。甚至他只有十塊錢而全部佈施，或是只剩下一碗飯吃，而佈施給真正需要的人吃。這種功德力才是無量大的。

　　First, doling money: this is a common way known by everyone. Sharing money and alms to those who really needed help is called charity. How much wealth you dole was not judge by the amount. For example, a person who donate ten thousand dollars while having ten million dollars property, and another person with a property of ten thousand dollars and dole ten dollars; the one who donate ten dollars had dole more than the one who donate ten thousand dollars. When a person had only ten dollars and he/ she donated that ten dollars, or he/ she had a bowl of food and doled it to those who were really in need; the power of merits and virtues were the most greatest and powerful.

　　二、勞力佈施：以歡喜心去幫助需要幫助的人做事。如做志工或幫助行動不方便的人過馬路。沒有分別心的幫助他人，就像

觀世音菩薩，普度眾生，把世上一切眾生，都看作是祂的子女，猶如父母親，對自己子女一樣慈悲，聞聲救苦救難。但是不可以有私情，而要覺破它，情見破除了、私情覺破了就成「大情」。私情是有情；大情是無情。覺破私情就是「覺有情」，又稱為菩薩。只要去幫助真正需要幫助的人，你就是菩薩。所以說：人要做菩薩也是很容易，只要沒有分別心地佈施勞力就可當菩薩。

Second, labor doling: help those who needed help with a true heart. Such as being a volunteer or help those disabled to cross the streets. The helping heart with no differences was like Guanyin, the mercy Buddha who prays for all people wishing them a good life in the previous, present, and future lives. She treated everyone as her own children, as if parents treating their kids with kindness and save those who suffered. However, you should not have private emotions, and had to look through it. Private emotions would develop into feelings. Private emotion is a sentient being, but feeling is merciless. Feeling over private emotion would become feeling with emotions. That is also called Bodhisattva (Buddhism term). You were a Bodhisattva while you help those who really needed help. Thus, it was easy for people to be a Bodhisattva. You just have to dole alms with a kind heart to anyone.

三、精神佈施：如有親朋好友或認識的人，在創業或遇到困難，給他鼓勵，增強他的動力。如果遇到不稱意的人就安慰他，讓他的心感受到溫馨。一句鼓勵、一句寬慰，對於失意的人來說都有著無窮的力量，這叫做精神佈施。

Third, spiritual doling: if your relatives or friends were having difficulties with doing business, you could give encouragement and strengthen his/ her motivation. Giving comfort to those who were in bad mood would let them feel warm. An encouragement or a caring would be a meaningful power to those who were in misery. This is called the spiritual doling.

　　四、語言佈施：讚美他人，可以使人開心。如遇到認識的人，就說好聽的話：「您今天看起來容光煥發，穿得很好看，年輕了好幾歲。」如見到或知道他人在佈施金錢或物質，就以嘉言稱讚他。稱讚佈施的人，自己也得到一半功德，像這種無本生意真好賺，其實佈施就這麼容易。

　　Forth, language doling: compliments could make people happy, such as saying good words when bumping into a friend on the street, "you look stunning today and you dressed so beautiful that you looked younger." We also compliment those who were doling out alms. Compliment those who dole would gain half merits and virtues. This kind of non-profit business was really an easy job. This was how easy doling out alms would be.

「寬容喜悅行佈施，安樂功德自心知。」
"We donate the toleration and the gratification; we know the peace, happiness merits and virtues"

分享比擁有更幸福

Sharing means more happiness than owning

及時行善

No haste in doing what is good

　　人降生來到這個世界裡，是來受苦又要還宿業債的，所以我從不慶祝自己的生日，我認為這是來受苦的日子。我的生日不舖張辦桌請客，節省下來的餐費，又可多認養幾個小朋友，以佈施報恩，來抵消宿業罪。同樣是花錢，但我佈施給需要的人，卻能使自己真正得到好處。

People came to the world to suffer and paid back from their previous lives. Thus I never celebrate my birthday because I think that is the day I came to suffer. I did not hold banquets on my birthday so the money saved could use to help more children in need. The good I gave could balance the crime or sin from my previous life. Same as spending money but I spend on those who really in need could do me real good.

　　在我的生活中，處理每件事情都跟做生意一樣，會很用心地去分析之後再做，這才不會浪費自己的資源和精力。其實佈施也不一定要花很多錢，回想我當兵的時候，只花了十塊錢買一張車票和兩個麵包給老奶奶，她就感激到眼淚掉下來。所以說只要付出一點點愛心，就算暫時吃一些虧，雖然金錢少了一點，但是日後必然能夠換來豐碩的果實。

I would handle everything in my life as if I was doing business. I would do things with my heart and think before I took actions. This would not waste my time and strength. In fact you would not have to spend much money to dole out alms. Recalling one time when I was serving in the army, I spent ten dollars for a ticket and two pieces of bread for an old lady. She touched with tears. We just have to show more of our love. Even though our money became less, or we lost something, we must gain more in the future.

好人自有好報。有愛心的人，一生都會得到別人的尊重，只要真誠的愛心，不管是多或少，只要盡了自己的力量去做，人生離世就沒有什麼可後悔的。但也有人雖然很想佈施，可是總說再等一等，過幾年我兒女長大，成家立業有基礎，能夠獨立了，我再來做。還有一些人說：我現在生活剛好過得去，等到我有了存款再做。

We would be treated well if we are nice to others. People with a kind and loving heart would win others; respect for the whole life. We have to treat others with true hearts, no matter how much, once we have done our best, there's nothing to be regret for. There were still some people who wanted to dole alms, yet they were always waiting for the time that their children to grow up and be independent. Some people would donate only when they have more savings left.

每天電視或報紙幾乎都有發生意外而死亡的新聞報導，還有些人過量暴飲而造成很年輕就得了重病。早期的人沒有東西吃而營養不良才生病，現在的人是吃的太豐盛而生病，甚至心肌梗塞或心臟麻痺馬上過世，可見死亡是不限年齡或貧富的，所以說佈施不能再等。我經常提醒自己，今天穿的拖鞋，明天起床不一定還有機會穿上它，這不是消極，而是確實如此。

There were accidents or death on the news every day, or people getting sick while they were young because of overeat. In the earlier times, people got sick because of eating too less food and malnutrition; now people got sick because eating too much. It would cause heart attack or heart failure and died. Thus death is not about age or rich and poor. We could not wait to dole out alms. I often remind myself that the slippers I wore today maybe I would not have chance to wear it next morning. This was not passive, it is the truth.

「及時行善種果因，佛光普照合家平。」
"We plant a karma and charity right now; God always shines in all directions and family will have a peace."

樂於助人
Happy to help others

　　子曰：「德不孤，必有鄰」。做人必須懂得朋友之道，眾多的朋友，往往是最有利於我們開創事業的資本。有了成就，絕對不可疏忽昔日的同事或朋友，如果他們到訪，我立即放下手上工作，親自倒茶招待，陪他聊天，不敢怠慢。

　　Confucius said, "A man of virtue can never be isolated. He is sure to have like-minded companions." People should understand the importance of being friends. Having many friends is always a good capital for business. We should never forget the old friends when we reached success. If a friend came for a visit, I would immediately stop my work, treat them with tea, and chat with them.

　　越有成就，對親朋好友態度就越要親切、更加謙虛，這樣友誼才會長存。自從離鄉背井至今，生活在多元化的社會，感受到與人之間的矛盾，有時候要做好人，幫助人家，可能會被騙，如不想做，心又會不安。所以，平常只要朋友或主顧遇到困難，我都會用心去評估，然後想出適當的方式去幫助他們，因此他們不會辜負我。不過，有時候也會遇到令我傷心又破財的事。

　　We should treat our friends more friendlily when we were more successful. Also, we should be humble and kind to keep the friendship last. Since I left my hometown for work, I experienced a diversity of life style, and felt the contraction between people. Sometimes we wanted to be good people and help others, but we might got cheated and wanted to quit. Due to the insecure feeling inside, I would not quit. Once a friend or a customer has difficulties, I would think twice and come up with the best way to help. Therefore, they would not disappoint me. However, there

were still some sad stories too that broke my heart and took my money.

那時有個主顧，我一次又一次幫助他，好話說盡還是沒用，到最後才放棄。他欠了幾個月貨款沒給，我照常出貨給他，勸勉他先付出艱苦的努力，然後才有收穫，凡事從眼前做起，從身邊做起，不要好高騖遠，不切實際的異想天開。

There was a customer that I helped him again and again, and eventually in vain, so I quitted. He owed some payments for months, but I gave him my products as usual. I gave advices and encouraged him to work hard first to gain more. We should not reach for what is beyond one's grasp and be impractical.

又鼓勵他認真經營，借了他現金周轉。他到約定時間都沒還款，還用心機買芭樂票來調現，最後我才知道他沉迷賭博。我依然勸勉他：「只要戒賭，我還是會出貨給你做。」到最後我又被騙了。其他還有幾個人一開始也和他一模一樣，沉迷賭博、喝酒，但是他們改過自新，所以最後有不一樣的結局。

I encouraged him again and lend him some money for turnover. He did not pay back at the date we agreed, but bought rubber checks for money. At last I realized that he had been obsessed with gambling. I still encouraged him to quit. I said I would still send out my products to him; however, he lied to me again. Some other people were like him before. They gambled and drank, but they had a new start. Thus they had a different future.

有個主顧，我跟他的互助會結束了，但他卻付不出欠我的會錢和貨款。我知道如果我硬要他還錢，他就沒辦法再營運，我就建議他這些款項暫時欠著，即日起再進貨的貨款要準時付清就好。幾個月後，貨款也沒付又跑掉了。我透過管道找他出來，再一次相信他，並且勸勉他：「你還年輕，又有妻兒要靠你生活，要負起男人責任，以前的帳款全掛著，我照常出貨給你再經營。」這次他真的做到了。二年後，他欠其他人的錢全部還清，家庭也很和樂。接下來他可以每月攤還以前欠我的貨款和互助會的錢，直到現在已經快還清了。

There was another customer who had a credit union with me. After the union was over, he had no money for the payment he owed me. I knew he could not do business anymore if I grabbed money from him. Therefore, I suggested that he owed the debit to me but from the day on, he should pay on time. A few months later, he did not pay anything and had run away. I tried to find him and wanted to trust him again. I encourage him, "you're still young, and your wife and kids depended on you. You should be responsible. Just forget the old payments first, and I will keep sending you products to do business." This time he really did it. He had paid me what he owed in two years, and lived happily with his family. Next, he could pay all he owed the credit union and I by installment. The payment has almost been paid off until now.

有一個主顧也是一樣的情況，連交通工具都賭掉了，也欠我很多貨款。那時他下定決心要認真做，想東山再起，但是他要買車才能夠再經營，因為他的行業必須有車代步。買車要分期付款，所以要請我當買車的保證人，我鼓勵他只要腳踏實地、改過自新，就當他買車的保證人。他真的沒讓我失望，三年後還清欠別人的債務，八年後還清欠我的債務，又買了一棟樓房，娶老婆又生子，有一個美滿的家庭。

One of the customers had the same problem. He even lost his car by gambling, and had owed me some payments. At that time he had set his heart firmly to work hard. However, he needed a car to do business. He needed to pay by installment for a car so he made me the guarantor. I promised to help him as long as he wanted to work hard and try hard again. He did not disappoint me. He had paid off the payment he owed to others in three years. After eight years, he paid back what he had owed me, and had bought a house. He got married and they had children in a happy family.

只要願意腳踏實地，東山再起，這樣的主顧，永遠是路特公司的客人。如果當時我嚴厲向他索債，他就沒辦法繼續做生意而倒閉。他欠我的錢，也不可能還，我又會失去一位主顧。所以說：常以寬容心待人，一定會得到好報的。我深切的體悟到，幫助人家而使對方有成就，這才是人生中最快樂的事。

As long as they wanted to work hard and try hard, they were always welcome as Root's customers. If I was harsh on them and wanted their money back, their business could not go on. The money they owed would not pay back, and I would also loss a customer. Therefore, treated people with a kind heart would always bring good effects to you. I strongly understand the true meaning of helping others and made others success. This is the happiest thing in life.

「好高騖遠不實際，腳踏實地靠自己。」
"It is unreal to reach for what is beyond one's grasp; it relies on myself step by step"

別忘了老朋友—不念舊惡

Remember old friends – let bygones be bygones

　　人非聖賢、孰能無過。有一個比較特殊的朋友，那是三十五年前之事。當時他在做生意。經常向我調現金，二人每天幾乎通電話談笑，算是非常好的朋友。他貸款買了一棟店面，資金更緊，幾乎每天跑三點半，我經常協助他度過難關，也因此二人關係密切，就這樣持續三年。

No one is perfect. To err is human, to forgive, divine. I have a special friend, and it was thirty-five years ago. At that time, he was doing business and had often dispatch cash with me. We talked on the phone almost every day and we were good friend. He had loaned for a store and was tight with his cash. He often went to the bank, and I helped him with difficulties frequently. Thus we became very close friend for three years.

　　當時不動產有一波漲價，他就賣掉三年前買的那棟店面，然後租店面做生意。賣掉這間店面賺了幾百萬元，當時銀行法規，要先還銀行貸款才能塗銷過戶給買方，他要我集資幫他先還清，等他賣店面的錢進來再還我。他賣掉店面的錢入袋後，立刻還我錢，並對我說：「我現在有錢了，我已經成功了，不再依靠別人來幫助。」想不到他會說出這種話！我以為他在說笑，但從那天起，也就沒有打過電話給我。我當然也沒打電話給他，君子絕交不出惡言，做一個有修養的人，無論何種理由，即使中斷來往，也應該寬恕他。既然雙方已經絕交，也就罷了，何必反目成仇呢？要避免樹立敵人，不記仇是一種美德。

The price of the real estate had rise so he sold the store he bought three years ago. Then he rented another store for his business. He earned a few millions by selling the store. The law said to paid off the loans in the bank to transfer the house to the buyer. He asked me for helping him to pay off the money to the bank, and he would pay me back with the money he earned from the rented store. After he sold the store successfully, he returned all the money he owned me, and said, "I have money now and I had succeeded. I do not need any help of others anymore." It was unbelievable that the words were coming out of his mouth. I thought he was joking, but he did not call me since then. I did not call him either. Gentlemen won't say bad things about a guy when breaking off a relationship. Being a wise man should always forgive others despite the fact that others had broken a relationship for no reason. The fact was a fact, and there is no need to be haters. To prevent being enemies, one must learn no to hold a grudge.

過了十六年，他來找我，說他急需要用錢，要我借他幾十萬。世事變化多，他今天還會來找我，真的讓我料想不到。既然他來了，我還是把他當做朋友看待，不念舊惡，畢竟以前不愉快的事已經過去了，過去的就讓它過去吧！他今天再來找我，從現在開始我們又是朋友。十幾年後，再見面的感覺，誠如孔子說的：「有朋自遠方來，不亦樂乎？」

After sixteen years, He came to me one day asking for a few hundred thousand in an emergency. Things changed during these years. I was quite surprised that he would come to me one day. Since he came, let bygones be bygones, I treated him as friend again. We became friends when he came to me. Seeing an old friend after sixteen years was like Confucius said, "Is it not delightful to have friends coming from distant quarters?"

真正的朋友，絕不在你失敗的時候不幫助你。孔子告訴子貢：「君子有成人之美。」自己好，也要成全別人好。所以，只要是對的事情，伸出熱情的手，予以大力幫助，使人度過難關，就都可以說是「成人之美」的「君子」行為，都是得人心、受歡迎的。人也要學會忠恕，才能懂得「己欲立而立人、己欲達而達人」的道理，意思是：自己想要有所作為，也盡心盡力的幫助別人，讓別人亦能有所作為；自己想飛黃騰達，也盡心盡力的幫助別人成功。

A true friend would help you whenever you have difficulties. Confucius once told Tzu Kung, "A gentlemen always helps people to fulfill their wish." We helped not only ourselves, but also others to make them better. Thus, as long as it was the right thing to do, give a hand and help others when they needed help would be a gentle behavior which achieved others' moral perfection. We should learn to be loyal and considerate to understand the moral of "If you desire to set goal as a benevolent person, you should help others to set theirs too". It means to help others in order to help oneself, and we need to help others succeed to be successful ourselves.

我今天能有一點成就，也都是受到一些朋友的照顧。朋友真正需要幫助的時候，如果我不去做，心裡會很難過。他看起來好像非常急需這筆錢，所以我就借給他。人不可能沒有過錯，只要改過就算好人。他來找我，表示他知道以前對我態度是錯的，我不念舊惡，所以原諒他。（常以寬容心待人，生活會安樂自在）

What I had today have to give credit to the help of my friends. If I did not help a friend in need, I would feel sad. The friend seemed to need the money real bad, so I lend some to him. People make mistakes, and the good ones corrected their errors for a new start. He knew his attitude toward me was bad so he came to me. I did not care about the old grievance so I forgave him. (Treated people kindly would brings you a happy life)

一個月後，他跟我調現的支票無法兌現，跳票了。生意無法再經營，結束營業。欠我的錢也沒辦法還，我也認了。他都一直避不見面，我透過管道告知他，錢不用還，但是也要常讓我看你呀！經過半年他才出現在我面前，我請他吃飯又勸勉他，也希望他有機會再翻身。再經過半年，他介紹一個朋友賣不動產給我，二年後不動產大漲，我也賺到了一筆錢。仔細想想，雖然他欠了我的錢沒還，我先吃了虧，可是到最後我才是大贏家。所以說：有捨才有得，如果念念不忘舊仇，好運就會被擋在門外。

One month later, the pay check he gave me had bounced and could not transform into cash. His business could not go on and he closed the store. He could not pay my money back and had refused to meet me. I find ways to tell him that he did not need to pay me money back; however, we needed to meet more often. He showed up after six months, and we went to a restaurant together. I encouraged him again, hoping that he could find a way to start over. After another six months, he introduced me a friend who was selling real estates. The price of the houses widely raised, and I had earned a lot from it. To think this over, even thought he did not return my money, I was the big winner in the end. Therefore, the hand that gives gathers. The good luck would be blocked outside the door, if we did not forget the old grievance.

「君子德行菩提心，寬恕助人福報臻。」
"A nobleman is morality and conduct as aspiration for Buddhahood; a nobleman is forgiveness and helping others then he receive the karmic reward"

量力助人是學問

Those who know their capability to help others are wise

　　子曰：「有朋自遠方來，不亦樂乎！」在社會上還是要有朋友。其實主顧和朋友如遇到困難，我都會想盡方法去協助他們。自從我有經濟能力幫助人家以後，就有一個想法：幫助真正需要幫助的人，是人生中最應該去做的事，也是最能得到快樂的事。不過，要注意的是眼睛要大點，量力而為，絕對不能超出自己的能力。其實解囊助人是一門大學問，風險也很大，要非常小心的仔細評估後，才斟酌盡善的去做。千萬記住，幫助朋友是好事，但是，一定要注意，不要讓他連累了自己。

　　Confucius said, "Is it not delightful to have friends coming from distant quarters?" It is important to have friends at work. I would try my best to help the customers or friends if they really needed help. I had a thought since I had the financial ability to help others: Helping those who really needed help is the thing we must do in life, and that is the way we receive most happiness. However, we need to know our capability and never do things beyond our capability. In fact, contributing one's fund to help others is quite a lesson, and it was risky. We have to be very careful after thinking clear enough to make the decision. Remember, helping others is a good thing, yet under the condition that we had the ability to do so.

　　現實的社會中以借貸金錢去幫助他人的情況越來越少了，因為幫助別人的風險太大了，所以有的人知道朋友經濟發生問題就遠離他。我童年生活在農村，又是困苦的家庭，曾經有貧窮的經驗，所以知道朋友有金錢的困難，我都會盡力協助他們。但也因為這樣吃了好多虧。不過我還是不放棄，幫助真正需要幫助的人，會覺得自己又做對一件事，心裡感受到溫馨、充滿喜悅、得

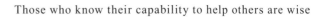

到安樂。

Today, lesser and lesser people would help others with money. It was too risky that some people would alienate those friends who had financial problems. I grew up in a farming family and experienced the poor life, thus I would try my best to help friends with financial crises. However, others took advantages of me, and I suffer many losses. I did not quit or gave up helping others. I considered it a right thing to do, and I would feel happy and warm inside my heart.

尤其幫助弱勢或殘障的人，更能體會到他們的善良。十幾年前，認識一對夫妻，他們是全盲的按摩師，開了一間按摩店，我常去找他幫我按摩，久而久之兩人變成好朋友。他做人處事很理性，所以我很讚賞他。有一天，他提起要我借他一百萬元，當時我有點驚訝，我們認識那麼久，從來不談金錢的事，突然要我借給他這麼多的錢，讓我百思不解。因此想先瞭解整個狀況之後，再決定是否要幫忙他。

Especially when helping the vulnerable or the disabled, I would feel their kindness even more. Ten years ago, I met a husband and wife who were blind massagists. I often went to the massage store they managed, and we became friends. They were rational people and I liked them very much. One day he mentioned about borrowing a million dollars from me. I was surprised because we never talked about money since we had met. There must be a reason that they asked for such a big number. I tried to understand the situation first then decide whether lending them money or not.

他說：「最近買了房子，已付了訂金，這幾天必須先付自備款，剩下的是向銀行貸款，雖然很早就把錢規劃好了，卻臨時出了狀況。因為以前借給朋友的錢要不回來，所以不夠支付自備款。我把錢借給朋友，他承諾我買房子之前，會把錢還給我，現在我買了房子，急需要用到這筆錢，他卻推說現在沒辦法馬上還錢。遇到這種事，真不知道如何是好？心裡非常著急，坐立難安，不知所措，所以你是否能幫我這個大忙。」

They said, "We bought a house recently, and had the deposit paid. The down payment needs to be paid these days, and we would loan from the bank for the rest. Even though we set plans for payments, there was a problem. We do not have enough money for our down payment since a friend did not return our money. I once lend some money to the friend, and he promised to return the money before we bought the house. Now that we bought the house, he had excuses that he could not pay me back at once. We really don't know what to do with this. This made us nervous and not knowing what to do. So could you help us with this big favor?"

我聽了以後，非常同情他的遭遇，自己也很單純，從沒想過把錢借給他人會有很大風險的。俗語說：「借錢歡喜臉、還錢苦瓜臉。」但是，我了解他是一個很守信用、行為端正的老實人，因此無息借給他一百萬元。我們約定，按月攤還給付，到目前為止快還一半了。有時候幫助真正需要幫助的人，心裡會有說不出的喜悅，這也是我人生的目標。

I was sympathized with what they had been through and had never thought about how risky it was to lend money to others. A proverb goes, "One smiles when borrowing money, and frowns when returning". I know him well that he was an honest man with credit, thus I lend him one million dollars without interest. We had made a deal that they returned the money monthly. They had paid back half of the money until now. Sometimes I would feel a sense of indescribable happiness when helping those who really needed help. This is one of my goals in life.

> 「解囊助人行好心，欣喜點燈照光明。」
> "We are kindness to help others and contribute money to charities;
> we are happy for lighting up then it illuminates all directions"

運隨心轉

The luck changes with the heart

好運就是好心情
Good mood brings good luck

　　好幾年前有一位朋友來找我訴苦說：她目前有一些困境，想要請人改運，我建議她，要請人改運的錢，不如去認養小朋友，這可能比妳花錢請人改運還好。她同意我的說法，很快就認養一個小朋友。經過幾個月她又來找我，說好像沒有什麼效果。她不了解因果，有如栽種果樹，要等它萌芽慢慢長大茁壯，然後結了果實，還要等到熟了才能享用。

Many years ago, a friend came to me to complain that she had some difficulties and wanted to change her luck. I suggested her that she should use the money on adopting a child instead of changing luck. That would be more useful than to change luck. She agreed what I had said and soon adopted a child. She came to me again few months later saying that it did not make any differences. She did not understand the effect. As if planting a tree, we had to wait until it grew and blossomed to taste the sweet fruits.

　　我告訴她，如果一個人得的病是慢性病，醫生給他藥吃，也要很長一段時間才會好呀！我問她，有沒有收到小朋友寄信給妳？她說有。我再問她，妳看完小朋友寫來的信，當時心情感受如何？她回答：感覺心情愉快，但是很快就過去，這也不能改變我的困境。

I told her if a doctor gave a chronic disease patient some medicine, it would take a very long time to heal the patient. I asked did she get the letters from the child, and she answered yes. I asked again how she felt when she received the letters. She replied, "I feel happy but the happiness faded away quickly. It could not solve my problems."

我又說：妳要把握住當時的快樂心情，不再讓它溜走，就留在妳心裡，遇到不如意的事，就回想起當時的好心情，這樣就是改運呀！妳如果花錢請人改運有這麼快嗎？她又說了，我要的是財，而不是無形的心情感受。

Then I told her, "You have to treasure the happiness at the moment and kept it from slipping away. Since you kept the happiness in your heart, you could remember the happiness whenever you feel sad. This is changing the luck. Would it be that effective if you spend money to change your luck?" She answered, "What I wanted was money, not the kind of virtual feeling."

可是一個人心情不好，做事情可能會做好嗎？財神要進來，見到妳愁眉不展，也會跑掉。一個人要有財富，先要做到心情愉快，如果財神爺經過妳家才會進來，每個人都喜歡和心情愉快的人做朋友，財神爺也一樣，妳保持心情愉快，就會有機會解決妳的困境，這不是改運嗎？

How could a person do things well with a bad mood? The God of wealth would be unwilling to help as long as he sees a frowning face. A person has to be happy to welcome the God of wealth. Everyone likes to befriend with the happy people, so do the God of wealth. Your problem would be solved if you keep being a happy person. Isn't this the change of luck?

「和氣生財自然來，佈施無求心愉快。」
"It is coming that friendliness is conducive to business success; it is joyful that we donate for others and have no requests"

笑臉迎財神

Welcoming the God of wealth with a happy face

　　我跟她又舉個例子：幾年前有個機緣，認識一對夫妻和他們的兩個小孩。他們曾經做生意失敗，也因此過得不是很稱意，但是他們每天做生意的時候，都很快樂的樣子，對客人很客氣，笑咪咪的，每次見到他們，不但他們心情好，我心情更好，久而久之就變成朋友了。

　　I told another example to a friend, "Few years ago, I had a change to meet a couple and their children. Their business was not very successful and they lived with difficulties. However, they were very happy when they were working every day, and they were nice and kind to their customers. The customers not only felt happy to see their smile, but also be in a better mood themselves. Soon the customers and the couple became friends."

　　他們的店面是租來的，後來房東告知要漲房租了，這次漲的幅度很高，他們準備另找個地方租。我就建議他們買自己的店面，不要搬來搬去，他誠實告知我：「我沒存款，哪來錢買店面？買一間店又不是買一件衣服，哪有那麼容易？我也很想呀！但是這是不可能的事。」

　　They rented the store, but the owner informed them that the rent had raised. Because the rent raised too high that they had decided to find a new place. I suggested that they bought the rented store then they would not have to move. They told me honestly, "I do not have any savings, and how could I buy the store? We're talking about buying a store, not clothes. How could it be easy? I wanted to, but that's impossible."

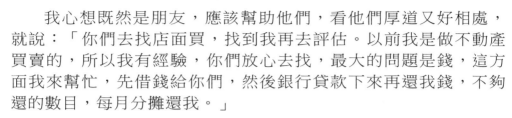

　　我心想既然是朋友，應該幫助他們，看他們厚道又好相處，就說：「你們去找店面買，找到我再去評估。以前我是做不動產買賣的，所以我有經驗，你們放心去找，最大的問題是錢，這方面我來幫忙，先借錢給你們，然後銀行貸款下來再還我錢，不夠還的數目，每月分攤還我。」

　　I thought I should help them as long as we were friends. They were nice and kind people. I said, "you go on to find the store and I will do the evaluation. I used to sell the real estate so I had experiences. You can take your time and search, and I will solve the biggest problem which is money. I'll lend money to you, and you could return the money after you got the loan from the bank. If the loan was not enough, could be paid back monthly afterwards."

　　那時銀行利率低，買的比租的划算。一個多月就找到適合他營業的店面。他請我去看那間店面，看了之後，我認為還不錯。我仔細的計算每月要繳房貸的錢，竟然比租店面還少了一點。他說：「如果沒有你幫忙付頭期款的話，這個店面再好也沒辦法買。」我心想既然這間店面適合他們，我就幫忙買下來。從簽約到過戶完成，我全部負責。一個月後這家人就搬進新買的店面營業。真的買的比租的還便宜，每個月少了七千元支出，就這樣在這店面營業四年，生意還可以。

　　The interest rate was quite low, so it was better to buy the house than to rent the house. They had found a perfect place for their store after one month. They asked me to evaluate the store, and I thought the place looked nice too. I summed up the house loan that they needed to pay each month, and it was lower than the rent. They said to me, "if it wasn't your help of the down payment, we wouldn't have bought the store no matter how great the place was." I thought I should help buying the store as long as it was a good place for them. I helped from signing the contract to the transferring of the ownership. They had moved in the new store and started their business after one month. It was really cheaper to buy the house than to rent the house. They had save seven thousand dollars each month and their business seemed fine for four years.

四年後房子漲價了，他跟我商量，如果現在把這間店面賣掉，可以賺七百多萬。因為以前他做生意失敗，還欠親人一百多萬，想趁這個機會賣掉，賺的錢可以還給親人，口袋又剩餘好幾百萬元。他再找個工作做，日子也會很好過，沒債一身輕。我聽他的建議也有道理，就說：「既然你們有這種想法也不錯，真的欠人家錢，心裡每天都會有負擔，雖然是自己的親人，也是一樣。」幾個月後他們真的賣掉了房子，賺了七百多萬元。

They house price raised after four years. They asked me whether it was a good idea to sell the store for seven million dollars, because they still owed their relatives one million dollars in their former business. They wanted to sell the house to return the money and get millions of dollars left for their savings. He could find a job so they would live well with no debt pressure. His suggestion sounded reasonable so I replied, "it's good that you thought this way. We often would not feel good inside while owing money to others, even if they were relatives." They sold the place and got seven million dollars.

我和朋友說，他們今天有這個機會賺到這筆錢，也是因為他們夫妻每天心情愉快對人厚道，財神爺才會進去幫助他們，所以說心情愉快好運自然來，妳認養的小朋友來信讓妳心情愉快，他們經常為妳祈禱，有一天總會運轉財神來，這是一個好的開始，請妳打開愉快心情等財神爺進來吧！

I told me friend that they would have the chance to earn money because the couple treated others kindly and they had good mood every day. God of wealth would be willing to help. Thus, the good luck would come as long as you keep yourself in a good mood.

Letters from the child you helped made you happy, and they prayed for you. One day the luck would change and your fortune would come. This was a good start, so please open your heart with a good mood to welcome the God of wealth.

　　態度決定高度，個性決定命運，一般的人常將無法掌握的事，歸咎於命運─命是宿世做過的因、運是今生受的果。其實命運與個性有極大的關聯。就如種豆得豆、種瓜長瓜的道理是一樣的，也是佛教所說的因果。所以我常提醒自己─修正個性，才能夠運轉命運。「若言下相應、即共論命運；若實不相應、合掌令歡喜。」

　　Attitude determined your altitude, and your personality determined your fate (luck). People often blame those unpredictable things on fate – fate is the cause from your previous life, and luck is the effect of your present life. In fact, fate has a close connection to personality, such as the moral of "As you sow, so you reap". This was the same as what Buddhist means "cause and effect". Therefore I often reminds myself – to change my luck, I should have a good personality. "If a person gets along with you, you could go on and talk to him/ her about fate; if the two of you couldn't agree with each other, just response him/ her with a smile but the two of you remain the happiness."

「怡然自得有福報，心寬好運貴人到。」
"When be happy and pleased with oneself we have a karmic reward; when not lend oneself to worry and anxiety the mentor brings a good luck"

助人莫望報

We don't request for returns when helping others

生命在呼吸間，生死在一瞬間，人如果三分鐘呼吸不來，生命就結束了，在這三分鐘的前一刻才想要做佈施，已經來不及了。所以說：愛不能等待，後悔來不及，呼吸不來無不空。我雖然是佛教徒，但是也非常同意道教的話。道教帝君有一段經文：「世道茫茫走西東，多少田園也是空，尋得名利珍珍寶，付與兒孫一場空，一旦咽喉呼吸斷，了了然然總是空，兒孫滿堂怎得見，黃泉路上不相逢，孽鏡上，憑過功，自己平生不修德，到頭何話見閻王，積些家業如珠寶，難贖冤愆上天堂。」

Life is between our breaths, but life and death fall in a sudden. People will die without breathing for three minutes. It would be too late to think of doling out alms before the last three minutes. Thus, we couldn't wait to love, and it would be too late to regret. Though I am a Buddhist, I understand morals of Taoism too. There was a scripture of a Taoism King goes, "we were busy about our life when we are alive. Getting lots of property and saving all treasures for our kids. When the time comes, nothing is exited. We won't know each other on the way of Yomi. We will be judged by Mirror of retribution. Wealth won't wash away our guilt. Without any virtues, how could we enter the Heaven?"

做人多少也要做一些好事，不然呼吸斷了，見閻王就沒功德可抵惡。

People should do some good things that they could balanced out the evil when seeing Yama, the King of Hell.

資助一個孩子也是一件功德啊！助人可使我們獲得豐盛的生命，也可能改變我們一生的命運。國人的習俗，如遇到挫折常會去算命或花錢改運，希望能夠轉運請來財神或保平安。我的觀念是不一樣的。我認為改運要靠自己改，花錢請人幫你改運是不會得到好處的。如果要花錢改運，不如把這些錢捐給真正需要的人，例如把錢捐給飢餓三十或認養小朋友。如果你認養了他，受益者的心靈就會和你緊緊連在一起，他對你有感恩之心，經常為你祈禱和祝福，你的運自然就會轉好。

To financially assist a child could be a virtue. Helping others could enrich our lives, and change our fates. From the custom of our country, that people would spend money on luck changing or fortune telling, then with that the change of luck would bring safeness and wealth. I have a different notion. I think that change of luck depends on us. Spending money would not bring any good to change your luck. To spend money on luck changing, we should donate to those who were really in need instead. For example, 30-hour famine or adopted a kid. If you adopted a child, the heart of beneficiary would be closely connected with yours. He/ she has a thankful heart toward you and they will often pray for you. In this manner, your luck would change.

但是千萬不可以先有期待運轉好之心，要順其自然，放下、不要求、不期望。幫助人家，心會感受到平靜、清淨、安逸、歡喜，自然而然就會得到好處，這就是給自己改運。

However, we could not expect a change of luck beforehand. Everything would occur naturally without request and expect. We would get the fortune by feeling peaceful, pure, and relax. This is the luck-changing of oneself.

「呼吸不來臨命終，財產積山也是空。」
"When no breathing we die; it is useless to hold a lot of properties"

自律的重要

The importance of self-discipline

好運會用完的
Good luck won't always exist

一生好的機運也許只有一次機會，如果沒有及時把握住，等到年老還是兩袖清風、雙手空空，為時已晚矣！隨時警惕自己。從前我做中古屋買賣的時候，鼓勵一位朋友買了我的房子，現金三十八萬，貸款一百二十萬。他這些錢是老婆早上在路邊賣飯糰、豆漿，下午到別人家裡做清潔工作，省吃儉用儲蓄而得來的。買了這間房子之後，他們整個家庭都非常高興，因為終於有了自己的窩。

The right chance or opportunity might come once in a lifetime. You would have nothing if you did not grasp the right moment. Then it would be too late to regret. Thus, we should always remind ourselves to be alerted. While I was doing the real estate business, I encouraged a friend to buy my house for three hundred and eighty thousand dollars cash with 1.2 million dollars loan. The money was all from his wife selling breakfast in the early morning and helped with the cleaning job in the afternoon. Their whole family was very happy after they saved their pockets on all the money for the house. They finally had their own house.

這間房子是四層樓公寓，位於台北市南京東路四段某巷子裡。住不到五年，時來運轉，突然有建商來談合作改建大樓之事。他考慮之後不合建，直接賣給建商，所得金額一千二百萬，還給先前向銀行貸款的一百二十萬，還剩下一千多萬。他這一生從沒料想到會有這麼好運的機會，但也沒想到一生僅有這一次好運，以後不再有了。

The house was a four-floor flat located in the lane of 4th section of Nanjing east road in Taipei. Not until five years that a company came to talk about a cooperating project for rebuilding the buildings. After consideration, he had decided not to join but sold the place to the company and got twelve million dollars. There was ten million dollars left after returning the loan (1.2 million dollars) back to the bank. He had never thought of having such good luck in life, and also had not thought of the good luck only occurred once.

他有了這一大筆錢，也就忘了以前老婆賺錢的辛苦。自從有了錢之後，整天無所事事，迷上了六合彩、玩股票。不到三年的時間，一千多萬全部輸掉了，又回歸到從前的環境，生活比以前還困苦。年紀越來越大，找工作更加困難。最後來找我，向我借了二十萬買了一部中古計程車來賺錢過日子，直到現在借給他的錢都沒還。可想而知，他一定很後悔沒珍惜這一生僅有的好機運，下一次的好運就要再等下輩子吧！有鑑於他貪心的教訓，我經常警惕自己。

Once he got the money, he forgot how hard his wife had worked for the money. He fooled around doing nothing and was obsessed with Mark Six and stocks. Not until three years, he lost all ten million dollars and got back to where he was at the beginning. His life was even worse than before. The older you got the harder finding a job will be. He came to me at last and borrowed twenty thousand dollars for a second-hand taxi to make a living. He did not return any money he borrowed. It was not hard to imagine how regretful he was not treasuring the one and only chance in his life. The next good luck will be in his next life. From his lesson of greed, I often reminded myself not to be like him.

雖然人皆有命運，是完全由自己在掌控的，好命或歹命，全決定在自己的平常為人處世的態度。即使是一個工人、職員、乃至於做生意或做任何事，全都是靠穩紮穩打的真功夫，不可能一步登天。凡事都要用盡心思，即使是枝微末節都要注意，一點一滴的累積經驗，這才能有所成就。容易得到的事物，就要更加珍惜，把握住機會，因為也許錯過這次好機會，這一生永遠再也遇不到了。所以遇到好事，要更加用心思考再去做，這可能是你這一生中命運的轉捩點，不要一失足成千古恨。

Though people have their own fate, it was actually controlled by us. Fortunate or not is totally controlled by the way we treated others. A worker, clerk, or a businessperson or even any other occupations should work hard practically. There is no shortcut to everything. Work hard and do the best on everything, even the tiniest trifles. Gaining experiences little by little could lead to a great success. We should treasure those that were easily-get, and grasp the special opportunity once in a lifetime. Thus, we should work hard whenever we encountered a good fortune. It might be the turning point of your whole life. Do not regret after lost.

> 「長者言下即是寶，勤儉無貪好到老。」
> "The older person's speech is treasures, it is good to end
> that we have industrious, thrifty and satisfy."

不要窮忙過一生

Do not let your efforts avail against nothing

　　「窮忙」這個詞耳熟能詳，很多人辛苦一輩子，可是到老還是雙手空空、兩袖清風。人的一生中不是沒遇到機會，而是自己不給自己機會，如果機運來了，就要把握住，按部就班、真心、勞心、用心、細心，不要讓它溜走。有些人一直很認真做，可是往往快要成功時，就差臨門一腳，終究功敗垂。如果沒有耐心，又吃不了苦，很容易就因此而退縮、被打敗了。就像工作遇到挫折就換工作；經營事業遇到瓶頸就不再經營下去。

　　The phrase "in vain" has been known to everyone, but many have worked in their whole life for nothing. It was us that did not give ourselves a chance, not fortune that we did not encounter. We should hold on to the opportunity whenever we had one, and be careful, patient, and work hard to keep it. Many people had worked hard but pity that they did not insisted to the last moment and failed to reach success that was just ahead of them. It would be easy for people to give up if having not enough patient and painstaking, such as transferring jobs whenever one encountered difficulties, or stop one's business whenever they failed.

　　「所謂天將降大任於斯人也，必先苦其心志，勞其筋骨」，唯有在困頓中，才能真正堅定心志。把握住年輕的黃金時間，學到技能，財源自然不竭而來。工商社會中，各行各業都有無數的競爭對手。俗語所謂：「三百六十行，行行出狀元」，就是在告訴我們，凡事只要實事求是，一步一腳印，最後一定能成功。經驗都是辛苦累積而得來的，如果經常換工作，只會浪費自己的時間，最後得不到利益。因為沒有堅持的毅力向前衝，就如出海捕魚的船隻，失去了動力漂流在汪洋大海中，最後又被拖回岸邊，徒勞無功，這不是窮忙嗎？

"When Heaven is about to place a great responsibility on a man, it always first frustrates his spirit and will, exhausts his muscles and bones." We could stronger our minds only in harshest surroundings. Grasp the golden period when we were young to learn skills, and the wealth would come to you surely. In the society of industry and business, there were countless competitors. There is a proverb goes, "There are three hundred and sixty trades, and every trade has its master." It means we would definitely succeed if we work hard and be practical. Experiences were gained from hard working. Transferring jobs is a waste of time and you would end up gaining nothing. Not having a will to consist is like a lost fishing boat in the sea. It would be dragged on shore with nothing gained. Aren't these all in vain?

今日用盡、明日求人。有些人賺到錢就不節制，玩股票、簽六合彩，其實只要是賭，到最後都是輸家。近幾十年來，一些親朋好友都抱怨說玩股票賺少輸多，到最後還是被大戶吃掉。不只是輸掉金錢，還賠了時間、精神。即使是退休老年人，每天把它當做是一種消遣，也需要衡量自己可以輸的限度，每天買一張彩券五十元就夠了，不要太過分投入，這樣才不怕輸掉家產。千萬不要將一輩子辛辛苦苦賺來的錢全部送給人家。如果迷了賭、玩樂又不節制，最後也是一個窮忙者。

Having nothing left today and asked for help tomorrow. Some people did not have the practice of saving money they have earned. They would spend money on stocks and Mark Six. Actually as long as you gambled, you would lose after all. During these decades, some friends had complained that playing stock was not a way to earn money because you would often lose. You would be swallowed by the big companies eventually. You would not only lose your money, but also bet on your time and mind. Even a retired old man had to balance the range of loosing if viewing stocks as a daily leisure. Buying a fifty dollar lottery everyday is enough. Do not over obsess with it to keep your savings. Also, do not easily give all you hard-earned money to others. If one has obsessed with gambling and could not control oneself, he/ she would be a person whose life was in vain.

　　自己窮忙一生，可不要連累子孫。四十年代，農村的女孩能夠讀完高中畢業，是非常少又難得的。村裡有一位大戶人家的女兒，她嫁給一位職位很高的公務員，當時算是門當戶對，雙方家世財富都不相上下。可是三十五年後，其丈夫留給兒子一筆債務。因為他相信自己很會玩股票，把近千萬的退休金，還有老婆的嫁妝｜一棟別墅都賠掉了，全部輸光光。最後剩下自己住的房子也向銀行貸款，還欠了百餘萬的卡債（今生枉費心千萬、退休空持手一雙）。兒子乖巧又聰穎，是公立學校碩士畢業，很想到美國再修幾個學分，因為必須揹負著父債，還有每個月貸款和卡債，而無法如願。如果過於迷了賭，不僅自己窮忙一輩子，又連累子孫，何不把退休金存起來，充分的利用它，一輩子安然自得、悠閒自在的生活，有多幸福呀！

We wasted our lives but do not waste our children's. In the 40s, it was very rare that a farm girl could finish high school. A daughter from a rich family in the village had married to a high-standard office worker. At that time they were meant to be with each other. The two families had similar fortune and wealth but the husband had left a great amount of debt to his son after thirty-five years. He believed that he was very good at stocking, and had bet on his ten million dollar pension and his dowry (a villa). Then he had lost them all. At last he had to loan for his own house and owed millions of credit card debt. (Wasting the hard work of life is nothing gained when retiring.) The son is smart and well-mannered master student graduated from a public school. He wanted to go to the states for further study but it was a dream that could not be achieve because of his father's card debt and monthly loan. Obsess in gambling not only kept your whole life wasted, but also kept problems to your grandchildren. Why not just save all the money and use them well to live a happy life?

　　久賭無贏家。賭、玩樂，每個人都很喜愛，我也不例外，只是要衡量自己的能力範圍再去玩，如果有損失，還保留了足夠積蓄可以生活過日子。辛苦賺來的錢是留給自己享用的，如果全部賭輸掉，贏家也不會向你說謝謝的，因此不要當一個窮忙者。現在年輕人要牢記在心，少壯不努力、老大徒傷悲，不可以心存僥倖。賭會耗盡精神，玩樂浪費時間，一定要把握年輕的黃金時間，去發揮自己的技能，先苦後甘，老了才有金錢依靠，就如六祖惠能大師所說的：「波波度一生，到頭還自懊。」

　　There is no winner in gambling. Gamble and feeling relaxed were lives that appealed to people, including me. However, we have to understand and control our abilities. If you lose all the money, the winner would not appreciate you. Therefore do not waste your time and put your life in vain. Teenagers must kept this in mind that you would not have to regret sadly when you were old if you worked hard while you were young. Do not think that we would have chances and luck. Gambling would wore out your mind, and fooling around would waste your time. We must treasure the time when we were young, and brought our skills into full play. We should suffer first to enjoy the happiness it brings, and then we would have enough savings when we were old. Just like Sixth Patriarch Hui Neng had said,　"Wasting time of your life would bring regret"．

「今生枉費心萬千，老年空持手一雙。」

"We waste more than thousands and myriads in my life;

when we are getting old we have only hands"

賺錢要用心、花錢多費心

Work hard to earn; think hard before you spend

　　古人說：「富不過三代」，真有其道理。有些人繼承了祖產，可惜沒好好善用而揮霍無度。因為錢不是自己辛苦賺來的，所以沒感受到賺錢的艱難。不知先人要費多少的心力、省吃儉用，才能省下來給子孫。有些人在很短的時間裡，就把先人財富花掉了，更慘的甚至導致家破人亡，後悔時已晚矣！真令人惋惜。

The ancients had said, "Richness won't pass on over three generations." That is a truth. Some people had inherited the patrimony but wasted it all. Because the money was not self-earned, people often could not understand the difficulties of making money. They did not know how much their ancestors had suffered and how hard they had worked to save the money for their grandchildren. Some people spent all the money they inherited in such a short time and even made the whole family destitute and homeless. It would be too late to regret. What a shame.

　　但若是自己賺的錢，其情況可就不同了。因為自己曾親身體驗到賺錢勞心又勞力的過程，想要花錢時，就會想到錢得來不易，所以每花一筆錢都會精打細算，避免浪費。詳細分析花這些錢值不值得、有何效益。反覆檢討之後再決定，因此會更謹慎的用錢。所以說賺錢要用心、花錢多費心。

However, it would be different with the money earned by us. We would learn difficulties of making money thus we would think twice before spending it not to waste the money. Think about whether it was worth the price and benefit before spending would be a better way to save money. Therefore, worked hard on making money, and think hard on spending it.

　　我每次想要花錢，腦筋就會不斷地去提醒自己｜賺錢不易，節省一點吧！工作非常辛苦，省點錢累積財富，未來生活才有保障。雖然花錢很高興，可是把錢省下來存入銀行，心裡安穩踏實又有安全感，也可以感受到存款的樂趣。所以花錢時，先想想是否有需要，才能充分享受自己的成果。

　　Whenever I wanted to spend money, I would remind myself that making money was not easy. I had to save money for my future life. Though spending money could bring happiness, I would feel secure and practical saving money in the bank. That is the fun part of saving money. Therefore, think twice on whether we truly needed it or not before spending it to taste our own fruitful achievements.

「富貴不知賺錢難，花光祖產時已晚。」
"When we stand on wealth and we don't know it is hard to earn money; it is too late that we spend patrimony"

腳踏實地

Be practical

　　生命的意義是什麼？每個人皆有不同的定義。可是認真賺錢是大多數人共同的目標和理想。沒錯！現在有錢才能生存，從踏出社會那一刻，大家就非常積極的找契機賺錢。

What is the true meaning of life? Everyone has a different definition, but working hard to make money is the shared goal and dream of everyone. That is right. We need money to live. Since the moment we step into society, we started to find ways to make money.

　　如果賺不到錢就要檢討自己，是否方法錯誤，或不夠專心，不肯勞心勞力做事。有些人賺到錢，可惜像過路財神，只經過而留不下來。辛苦賺來的錢應該要珍惜善用它，常提醒自己，錢得來不易。

We review ourselves whether that the method was wrong, or we did not try hard enough that we did not make money. Some people made money like the Passing-by wealth God which the money did not last long. We should be careful on the money we earned and often remind ourselves that making money was not easy.

　　當你賺到錢後花錢的觀點差異也很大，有的人，先犒賞自己；有些人，會先規劃，善盡管理使用。還有些人把錢送給別人（賭，就是其中之一），因為想要以捷徑賺更多的錢，所以一眨眼，昔日辛苦賺來的錢就轉給別人享用。

People would have different perspectives once they made

money. Some would treat themselves first, and some would set a plan on how to use the money. Some would give away their money to gambling. They wanted to make more money through shortcuts so with a blink of the eye the money they made would be others'.

　　如果賺錢很容易，大家就不必要這麼辛苦去賺錢。就是因為錢得來不易，所以要多善用財富，而且更要珍惜每一分錢。賺錢要用心，花錢更要費心。好高騖遠，不切實際追求財富的人到處都有，但能以輕鬆而不付出勞力的方法就得到財富的人，並不多見。我還是選擇一步一腳印、腳踏實地，有多少錢做多少事，才不枉費心萬千，空持手一雙。

　　People would not have to work so hard to make money if making money is so easy. Because money was difficult to earn, we should be more careful on using it and to cherish every dollar. Work hard on making money, and think hard on spending money. Do not reach too high for impractical things and wealth. People did that often but there were few people who could make money easily without efforts. I would choose to be practical and made every step firmly stable. Do what your money could afford to keep your hard work and you would not lose everything.

「勞力賺錢自有道，警惕珍惜樂到老。」
"We use the good method and our labor for earnings; when cherish and treasure our own we are happy in the end of life"

感恩——莫忘本

Be thankful and grateful

尋人啟事

A reunion with old colleagues

當我有了一點點成就，心中常想起昔日的老同事對我的恩情，不知該如何去報答他們。因為大家已經分開將近四十年沒見面了，為了自己的生活，各奔前程，這也是每個人一生中都會經歷過的情況。

While I was quite success, I would often thought of the times with my old colleagues and did not know how to thank them. We have been apart for forty years, working hard for our own live and future. This is what we would all been through in our lives.

現在我規劃要如何去做這件尋人啟事的工作，我試問其他幾位還有連絡的同事，他們的回答皆是：這是不可能的事，猶如海底撈針，到哪裡找？其實他們的回答也不是沒道理，可是我懷著一顆堅定、感恩的心，希望能有機會再次感謝他們。

I was planning on how to find my old colleagues. I asked some colleagues who were still keeping in touch, they answered, "That is like seeking a needle in the haystack. Mission impossible! Where could we find them?" Their answer had its reason, but I was firmly in the thankful heart to find them.

如果以前沒有他們的照顧，就沒有今天的我，想到這裡，又增加了許多動力，誓言一定要達成目標。我利用很多種管道，結果花了三個月的時間才找到二個人，比起做生意時自己當外務找客人還要困難。

If it was not their help, I would not have what I had today. Thinking of this gave more motivation to me. I told myself that

I will do it. I find many ways to reach the old friends, but I connected only two in three months. It was harder than finding customers when I was doing business.

借重這二位老同事的因緣再去找更多的人，心想著，就以一個人負責最少找二個人的方式，不到半年的功夫，被找到的老同事愈來愈多，有了正確的通訊資料近百位，我非常興奮能夠找到這麼多人，連自己也難以相信。

I thought maybe I could find more colleagues through the two colleagues that I had already reached. They could find at least two friends each, and more old colleagues were reached within 6 months. We got nearly one hundred pieces of contact information. I was so happy that we could find as many. I could hardly believe.

從我聯繫的過程中，感受到大家的心情都很激動，都抱著非常期待的心情，希望很快就可以再見面了。我當然很快就安排好宴會的場所，第一次受我邀請的老同事共計來了八十幾位，見面的當下有如親人分離了幾十年而再重逢的情景，有的人因見面激動到眼淚流下來。

During the process that I contact everyone, I could feel that they were very excited and eager to meet each other. I certainly arranged a place to meet up. There were eighty old colleagues, and we were so happy to see each other like a parted family that finally reunited. Some people were too happy that they burst into tears.

每個人有說不完的話題，宴會廳上充滿樂融融的境相，在每個人的臉上都看得出喜氣，好像自己家裡在辦喜事一般。其實最高興的人是我，讓我能有機會再次見到他們，能感謝他們，在我一路走來的扶持與幫助。

There were too much to talk about. The restaurant filled with happy atmosphere and you could see happy smiles on everybody's face. Actually I was the happiest one. Thank to them that I could meet them again and truly thanked them for what they had did to me along the way.

「生命意義互關心，相逢敘舊最溫馨。」
"When we can take care for others we know the meanings of life; we feel warm when we meet old friends"

父母恩重如山

The great love and kindness of our parents

　　父母恩情如山那麼高大，這是在學校常聽到老師的教訓。「養子方知父母恩、立身方知人辛苦」：自己在教養子女時，才感受到父母的辛勞，才知道恩情有多麼偉大。

　　Teachers often told us the great love and kindness of our parents. "You will understand your parents' love when you raise your own children. You will understand the difficult of a situation when you are standing there by yourself". Not until we raise our own children that we understand the great love of our parents.

　　孝順父母是天經地義、也是身為人最應該去做的事，更是做人最基本之事。孝順父母的人會有福報，尊敬長輩會遇到貴人相助。這跟種瓜得瓜、種豆得豆的道理是一樣的。

　　Showing piety to our parents is what we should do. It is the basic manner. We would receive karmic reward (good luck) if we show piety to our parents, and those who show respects to elders would be helped in needed. This is like the story of "As you sow, so shall you reap".

　　有俗話說：「孝於親則子孝、欽於人則眾欽」。孝順父母的人，將來子孫也會孝順你；不要怕吃虧，先尊敬別人，自己自然也會被尊敬。如同利益他人，有捨就有得，所以要先付出，將來一定能得到好處。

　　A proverb goes, "As you respect your parents, so do your son. As you respect others, so will others respect you." Your grandchildren would show piety to you if you respect your parents. You would also receive respect if you respect others, as if benefiting others. You will gain after giving.

又有人說：「樹欲靜而風不止、子欲養而親不待」。樹想要安靜不動，可是風卻吹得樹搖晃不停；做子女的想奉養父母時，可惜父母已不在人世，就算付出最大的心意，也無法再奉養父母了。

There was another saying, "The tree wants to be still but the wind is blowing; the son wants to show his respect but his parents have gone". The wind is blowing while the tree wanted to be still, and the parents were gone while the sons and daughters wanted to show their respect. Even if showing their deepest respect and love, they parents were no longer there.

我從小就遠離父母，雖然每個月都有寄錢回家給他們當生活費，可是鮮少回家陪著他們長住。所以現在想起來，我自己內心感到非常的愧疚、後悔、傷心、難過，仰頭無語問蒼天，時已晚矣！

I was away from my parents since I was little. Though I send money back for their daily supplies, I did not often go home to live with them. I would feel so ashamed, sad, and guilty every time I thought of that, but pity it was too late.

「孝順父母種善因，耀祖光宗子孫興。」
"Good actions lead to good rewards that we show filial obedience or devotion for our parents; it can prosper my ancestors and descendants"

因為感恩，所以行善
Being thankful and helped others

　　回憶三十年前，我生病送進台大急診室，醫生說：「無藥可治，生存機會渺茫，只能靠你的福報。假如有機會再恢復健康，這種病依我們臨床經驗，最多也只能再活十年。」當時祈望自己能夠慢慢恢復過來，如果只能再活十年，我也心滿意足了。

　　I remembered the time thirty years ago when I was in the National Taiwan University Hospital, the doctor said, "It was hopeless, and you could hardly survive. It all depends on your luck. If there's a chance to live, to our experience, you have ten years to live." I was wishing that I could recover, and I would be satisfied with only ten years.

　　來到台北的時候年紀還很小，一直受到很多人幫助、照顧、疼愛，感受到人間的溫馨。其實今天我有一點點成就，都歸功於昔日同事的幫助，我常常感恩，記在心裡。如果知道幫助過我的人，不管他有多大的困難，我都會義不容辭地去幫助他解決問題。

　　I was young when I first came to Taipei, and I felt warm, caring, and help. I am deeply thankful in my heart of the old colleagues for what I had today. I would help them with all I could to solve their difficulties.

　　想起以前一位同事的不幸，我的心裡就非常地難過。他經營事業失敗了沒多久就往生，他的老婆人很好，又有道義，她知道她老公向我借了幾十萬元沒還就走了，因此她想辦法要把錢還給我。當時聽到這句話我感到心酸，她能有這種想法使我感動到流下眼淚，我立刻告訴她，我欠她老公的恩情比這些錢還要多的

多，請她放心，不要再提起錢的事，如需幫忙也請告知，我會盡力而為。

I recalled a misfortune of a former colleague which made me sad. He passed away soon after he had filed his business. His wife is a good person with a kind heart. She knew her husband owed me some money and has wanted to return it back. I felt touch when she told me so. I told her that her husband's kindness was far more important than the money. I told her not to worry about the money and should never bring up anything about money again. If she needed any help, I would do my best to help her.

到現在為止，我多活了三十幾年，我常常覺得，可能是老天要留著我去幫助真正需要幫助的人，我欣然接受。我非常感激老天讓我有機會多活了三十幾年，反正多出來的時間，可以去做些更有意義的事情，才算是報答老天給我活下去的機會。

I have lived more than thirty years. I thought God wanted me to help others who really in need, and I accepted it. I was appreciated for the thirty years so I could do more meaningful things. I sincerely thank God for giving me this opportunity to live.

「立志忠實說道理，夫子教話講仁義。」
"It has a reason that it is faithful to make a resolution; the Confucius said that the benevolence and righteousness are necessary"

取諸社會，用諸社會

From the society to the society

感恩台灣世界展望會
Thanks to World Vision Taiwan

　　童年生活在農村，看到大部份村民都過著非常困苦的日子，有的人常需要別人幫助才能過生活，自從離鄉背井到台北，已經四十幾年了，記憶猶新。

I grew up in the countryside and understood the tough life on the farm. Many people needed help from others to live every day. I still remember the scene since I came to Taipei for forty years.

　　當時除了基督教會，偶而舉辦盛大聚會的同時，以麵粉救濟最貧困的人。得到麵粉的人都非常地珍惜又高興，因為可以吃到麵餅。所謂麵餅是以麵粉加清水，兩手用力扭轉、壓擠、絞乾，然後放進鍋爐煎，就成麵餅。一家人每個人只分得一塊，是當做一餐的飯食，而不是吃點心喔！

Except the Christian churches, I would dole out pack of flour in the big gathering parties we held. Those who get the flour would be happy to have the flatbread. The so-called flatbread is to add in water to the flour and then squeeze and fold. It would be flatbread after fried. A family member would get a piece as a meal, not dessert.

　　當我長大才瞭解這是所謂行善事，亦叫做善心的人。我再更進一步去探索，又得知四十年代起，台灣世界展望會就在台灣資助很多家庭渡過困苦的日子。我小時候也很貧窮，所以這些事烙印在我心。

I understood this was helping other when I grew older. I did further researched to understand that the World Vision Taiwan had financially assisted many families in their tough days. I had the same tough experience when I was little, so this had a deep impression in my heart.

　　當我被生出來的時候，全身光溜溜的。現在我擁有的財產、金錢也是從社會得來的。細心思考，徹底分析，生來本無一物，如果我比一般人多出的財富，也是社會多給我的。所謂「取諸社會，用諸社會」，回饋社會本就理所當然，是應該去做的事，沒什麼值得驕傲的。

I had nothing when I was born and now the wealth I got was from the society. I thought carefully that we born with nothing. If I had more wealth than others, it was from the society. "We took from the society, and we used what the society gave", so it was right to give feedback to our society. It was what we have to do, so there is nothing to be proud of.

　　今天我有一點成就，都隨時提醒自己，我應該要去幫助一些真正需要幫助的人，生來無一物，死後也無一物。我用不完的東西，死後也帶不走，還不如趕快拿出來幫助有需要的人，這是我人生的目標也是理想。

I was quite successful today but I often reminded myself that I should help those in need. We born nothing, and we die nothing. I could not bring what has left when I died; instead, I should use them to help others. This is my life goal and my dream.

「博愛仁心救世人，耶穌基督賜安平。」
"It rescues people with indiscriminate love and kindness; Jesus Christ gives us a peace"

橋樑─台灣世界展望會
The bridge - World Vision Taiwan

　　當我要幫助人家的時候都很小心，萬一被騙了，會傷害自己又會害了騙人的人。如果被騙徒得逞，他一輩子不想工作、不求上進，只想輕鬆騙人、不勞而獲，這對他是一種壞事，所以有愛心也要睜大眼睛。也因此我都找財團法人或有公信力的慈善機構。

　　I was really careful when I helped others in case that I got taken in. Both of us would suffer if I got cheated. Cheaters would not want to work again because he/ she would thought it was an easy job to get what they want. This was bad for them, so we have to be careful while we help others. Thus, I like those charity organizations with credibility.

　　我雖是虔誠的佛教徒，但因為助人是不分種族或宗教信仰，所以我認養了五十幾個世界各國的小朋友。這些小朋友都是透過國際級的台灣世界展望會，協助認養的。有台灣世界展望會來當我的橋樑，這對自己有保障，一定不會被騙。

　　I am a devout Buddhist but helping others is non-religious and regardless of human race. I adopted over fifty children all over the world. The children were adopted through international World Vision Taiwan. As long as World Vision Taiwan to be the bridge between kids and me, it would not be a problem.

　　每年我都會收到好多小朋友的祝福信件，每一次收到小朋友為我祈禱和祝福，心裡就感受到清淨、安樂、充滿喜悅，生命就會更有意義。像這樣利人又利己的好事，還能等待不做嗎？世人用盡心思去賺錢，但如何花錢是有益而又不浪費的，恐怕知道的人很少。

　　I would get many cards from the children every year, and feel happy, pure and warm every time I got the cards. I felt my life more meaningful. Why hesitate doing this while it benefits both others and us? People tried so hard to make money, but few has known how to spend money in a benefit way and waste not.

經常聽到有人說：「我又亂花錢了！」浪費錢似乎已成為現代人的通病。花錢應該要精打細算，避免浪費，例如少買一些可能不常使用到的物品，或少到娛樂場所，還可省一點點錢。要知道，少浪費一點點錢，就能幫助一個真正需要幫助的小朋友上學和得到飽暖。

I often heard people saying "I spent too much money again!" wasting money seemed to be a common problem now. We should think twice before we spend money not to waste it. For example we could buy less on things we seldom use or spend less time in the amusement places to save money. We could help a child to go to school or kept them away from hunger if we wasted less money.

所以說花錢做善事和做生意是一樣的，賺錢要用心，花錢做善事要多費心，這才不枉費工夫又浪費自己辛苦賺來的金錢。每捐一筆錢都要注意，是否真正為弱勢者解決問題。要用努力賺來的錢幫助真正需要幫助的人，這才是真的做了好事。不要以為把錢隨便捐了就是做好事。有心做善事，也要多用心。

Therefore spending more money on charity is like doing a business. We tried hard to make money, and we also work hard to do charity or help others. This would not be a wasted on the money earned. We have to be careful on whether the money was truly spent to solve problems of minorities. Using money we earned by working hard to help those who truly in need is doing good thing. Randomly donated money to some organization was not helping others. If we want to help others, we should try our best to help.

「先勝教化學道義，宇宙人生修真理。」
"We learn morality and justice before education;
we study truth in the universe and life"

拋磚引玉—愛不能等待—前台灣世界展望會杜會長

Get the ball rolling - Don't hesitate to love - Mr. Tu, The former president of the World Vision Taiwan

在每一個喜慶日子，我都會付出一點點心意。例如：我兒子結婚喜宴所收到的禮金，我透過台灣世界展望會轉交給需要幫助的小朋友。台灣世界展望會杜會長在宴會現場代表接受禮金。

I would devote my kindness in helping others once in a while during holidays. For example, I would give the cash gift from my son's wedding to children in need through World Vision Taiwan. The president of World Vision Taiwan accepted the cash gift at the banquet.

我做這件事只是想拋磚引玉，喜宴上大家吃得非常開心，可是我會想到世界上還有很多人沒飯吃，因此做了這件應該去做的事。取諸親友，用於需要幫助的小朋友，這次功德是屬於親友的，取諸親友而做慈善，所以對大家來說是功德一件。

I did this to catch a whale by throwing a sprat. Everybody had a good time at the banquet, but I thought of people who were hungry with no food to eat. Thus I did what I should do. I used the money from relatives and friends to the children, so the credits should be theirs. To them, they had done a good thing.

我是利用我今生難得的機會幫忙宣導慈善工作，這使我們整個家庭的紀念日更具意義。前台灣世界展望會杜會長說得好｜愛不能等待！國內外許多貧瘠、落後的角落，還有無數在貧窮匱乏中煎熬的兒童。大部份的家庭收入，每天不足一塊美元，這些孩子沒有機會上學，甚至有些孩子活不過五歲的生日。因為一個及時的愛心善念，一個可敬的資助行動，讓這些生活在艱困環境中的孩子能夠順利的上學去，能夠健康的成長，有機會迎向更寬廣、更豐盛的生命！

I used a special opportunity to promote the charity, and that made the anniversary more meaningful. I totally agreed to what the former president of World Vision Taiwan had said: "Don't hesitate to love". There were slums all over the world in every corner, and there were children suffering every day. Most of their families made less than one US dollar every day, and their kids had no chance of going to school. Some children even did not live over their fifth birthday. Just a kind thought at once or a respectful donation could make a big difference to the kids, or they could even go to school and live healthy. They could have the chance to live a powerful and meaningful life!

貢獻一己的能力為大眾謀福利，為人類多做有益的善事，多關心這個世界需要幫助的人。生命在呼吸間，生死在一瞬間，人如果三分鐘呼吸不來，生命就結束了，在這三分鐘的前一刻才想做善事，已經來不及了。杜會長說得很好：愛不能等待，後悔來不及，真的很有道理。

Contributing one's ability to benefit others, and do more things kindly like to care about those who really needed in the world. Life falls between our breath, but life and death fall in a sudden. People would die without breathing for three minutes. It would be too late to think of doing kind things before the three minutes. President Tu was right. Do not hesitate to love, or it would be too late to regret. That really does make sense.

「致予世人博愛心，浩然正氣慈善行。」
"We give people for indiscriminating love; we practice our affectionate love for awe-inspiring righteousness"

擁有全世界的感受
Having the feelings of the world

受到資助的小朋友，都會寫信問候資助人。小朋友寄來的信都寫的非常天真、可愛又令人感動。例如：

「謹奉主耶穌基督奇妙之名向您請安。我母親非常感激您對我的幫助，我很開心也愛您，我每天都跪下來為您禱告，願上帝隨時著保護您，愛您的孩子敬上。」

在那麼遙遠的地方，小朋友和家人都為我祈禱，我感到非常幸福。只要每天能節省一點點錢，節約一點能源，就能為一盞快要熄滅的油燈加點油，使它可以繼續再發光。我可以對自己說，我又做對了一件事，這也會帶給自己快樂，不是嗎？

The children who received donation would write letters to their donors. The letters from the kids were very adorable and touching. For example, one child wrote:

"I give my best regards to you in Jesus name'. My mom appreciates what you've did to me. I am happy and I love you. I pray on my knees for you every day that God always protect you. From a kid who loves you."

I feel love from afar where children and their family were praying for me. Just save a little money and resource every day, we could light up a lamp that is about to go out, and keep it shine for a while. I could say to myself that I did another thing right again. This would bring happiness, wouldn't it?

「我在史瓦濟蘭很好，希望您平安快樂，感謝您寄給我美麗的卡片和相片，我非常喜歡。我覺得很可愛也很引以為傲。我把它擺設在我母親的桌台上，每天都可以見到您。即使我們距離遙遠，我深深感受到您對我的關愛。我與母親在此致上誠摯的問候，願上帝保佑您和您的家人，謝謝！愛您的孩子敬上。」

看了小朋友的來信，感受到的幸福是不能和金錢來衡量。他們的真心，使我非常開心，更有精神去做事。今天事業有一點成就，小朋友給我的精神支持也有關係，所以我也很感激他們。

"I'm fine in Swaziland. Wish you happy and well. Thank you for sending me beautiful cards and photos. I really enjoy them. I think they're cute and I'm proud of having them. I put it on my mom's table so I could see you every day. Even though we're far away, I could deeply feel the love from you. My mom and I send our best regards and may God be with you and your family. Thank you! From a kid who loves you."

Reading letters from the kids, I understood that happiness doesn't depend on wealth. I was touched by their true hearts, and had more power to accomplish more things. Those kids were one of the reasons that I was quite successful on my business today, so I greatly appreciated them.

「這是從蒙古布爾省所捎來的問候，但願這封信在這個美好日子，為您捎來溫暖的祝福！您好嗎？我非常感謝台灣世界展望會，提供了一台輪椅給我的殘障女兒，我們非常開心，願您的生活順心、快樂！」

如果一個人在行動不方便的時候，突然有人幫助而改善情況，一定非常的高興，沒有經歷過的人，是無法體會的。

"This is from Boolean province, Mongolia. Hoping that this letter would bring happiness to you in this beautiful day. How are you? I appreciated World Vision Taiwan that offered a wheelchair to my disabled daughter. We were very happy. Wish you happy and well."

If we helped to improve someone's problem of walking, he or she would be extremely happy. People could not understand this unless they have some experiences of giving.

「我跟我的家人帶給您溫暖的祝福，您在台灣過的如何呢？我在南非很好，非常感恩您的資助，我才能夠繼續去上學，每天我都走路去上學。台灣天氣如何呢？感謝您成為我的資助人，愛您的孩子敬上。」

只要付出一點愛心，就能讓他有機會去上學，這對他的將來一定有很大的幫助。做這種善事，好像培育一棵樹，有一天長大了，也許是一棵大樹可供人乘涼，想到這裡我內心常感到欣喜。

"My family and I bring warm wishes to you. How are you in Taiwan? I'm fine in South Africa, and I'm thankful of your help so that I could go to school. I walked to school every day. How's the weather in Taiwan? Thank you so much for being my patronage. From a kid who loves you."

They could go to school if you give more love. This would be a big help to their future. Doing this was like planting a tree. The tree could provide a shady spot when it grows tall. It made me feel happy and excited.

「親愛的資助人您好：您給我的禮金已經收到了，非常謝謝您的資助，我會把錢買文具用品或拿去繳學費，我一定不會亂花的，因為這是您愛心的幫助，讓您破費真不好意思。您的心意已在冷冷的冬天裡帶給我溫暖，送您我親手做的玫瑰花一朵，它代表我的祝福與感謝，我也非常喜歡您喔！感謝上帝安排我可以認識您，這是我的榮幸，祝新年快樂，萬事如意。」

小朋友沒有錢又沒辦法賺錢，雖然我只資助他們一點點錢，這對一個真正需要的人來說，卻有很大的幫助。收到這麼感人又貼心的信，心裡感受到溫馨，使我得到無限的安慰。

"Dear patronage, I had received your cash gift. Thank you very much. I would spend the money on stationery or tuition. I would not waste them because it's your love. Sorry that you have to spend so much money. Your kindness had brought me warm in the cold winter. I sent you a handmade rose to show my thankfulness and best wishes. I like you very much. Thank God for letting us meet. This is my honor. Happy New year, and hope everything goes well."

The children have no money and could not make money. Though we helped them with little money, to them, those who were really in need, it was a great help. Receiving such touching letters, I felt so warm inside. This gave me a lot of comfort.

「萬事善緣自安排，事事如意心常開。」
"It is arranged that all things are relied on good karma; it is happy that it has all one's wishes"

感恩的心

A thankful heart

利益他人

To benefit others

　　生命去創造自己，每個人皆是如此。可是需要利益他人，就很多人有不同的觀點。辛苦而獲得的，為什麼要給他人呢？其實不然。

　　Life is to create oneself, and everyone is the same. However, when it comes to benefit others, people would have different perspectives. Why should I give away something that I fought so hard for? In fact, this is not the case.

　　有捨就有得，大家皆知道這個道理，可是要先付出去，內心一定會有掙扎。先捨，萬一沒回收，那豈不是吃虧了嗎？

　　Everyone knew that we gain after we give. Since we have to give before we gain, people often hesitate. What if I did not gain any after I give?

　　人是有感情的，只要對人好，以真誠的心去對待任何人，不要有分別心，更不可以瞧不起窮人，最後應該會得到好報。對人好而常記在心裡，這表示自己不常做利益他人之事，可不要做利益他人之事就牢記在心。

　　People have feelings. As long as we were nice to others and could not look down on the poor, we would receive good fortune after all. People who did not often help others would remember what they had done. We should not keep in mind when we help others.

　　不一定要以物質去利益他人，也可以用語言佈施或精神佈施。只要每天遇到人就說好話，一直持續下去，總有一天一定會發現周遭的人皆對你很友善。這也是因果論，有因就有果。需要人家幫助是無法預料之事。所以先種善因，如有急事，一定會有人伸出援手。假如得罪一個人，就多樹立一個敵人。多一個朋友，就多一個生意機會。

Not only donating objects could be counted as doling alms. We could also dole in speech or in spirit. We say nice things to people every day and keep it going, we would find that people around you actually treats you well too. This is also cause and effect. The cause leads to the effect. It is unpredictable when we needed help. Thus we need to plant good cause just in case. Someone would definitely give a helping hand. If we offend someone, we build another enemy. If we build more friends, we would have more business opportunities.

如果是做生意的人，更要先將利益給予他人。因為他得到你的友善，如有生意機會，一定幫你介紹。有位朋友曾經告訴我，利益他人真的是利益自己。他有位鄰居，以前很少互動，有一天開始對他善言（語言佈施），不到二個星期，這位鄰居就介紹一個工程給他做。所以說不要怕吃虧，利益他人就是利益自己。

People who ran business should first benefit others. Others would introduce you to a business opportunity if they get your help first. One friend had once told me that benefiting others is benefiting you. He has a neighbor who he seldom interacts with. One day he speaks kind words to the neighbor (language doling). Not until two weeks that the neighbor introduced a project to him. Therefore do not afraid to be in a disadvantage, because benefiting others is benefiting you.

「甜言一句有好報，善意利人記得牢。」
"When you said sweet words your charity would be rewarded;
it will be remembered for a good intention and benefit"

回首來時路─夢想成真

Glimpsed back the path - a dream come true

　　我今生的命運很多過程和一般人不同，一生中有過三次面臨死亡的經驗，而且每次都非常驚險危急。可是到了緊要關頭都會有奇蹟出現，而讓我能夠多活了幾十年。直到現在有時候回想當時面臨死亡的情景，還會膽顫心驚，全身冒冷汗。而我一生中做了三種連自己也料想不到的事業，到最後不但沒讓自己失望，而且還很滿意。

The fate of my life was very different from others'. I had three experiences of facing death, and all three of them were urgently desperate. However, there were miracles in the last moment so that I could live more than ten years. I would shiver and tremble when thinking of these situations. Also, I have done three unbelievable businesses, and I did not let myself down.

　　六十年代很多人對不動產買賣都很陌生，而且我是來自農村，更不瞭解買賣過程，我能夠突破種種的困難而賺到錢，這也是個奇蹟。而像我這樣連交流電、直流電都不懂的人，後來竟能做高科技產業，並且做得有聲有色，全台灣銷售量第一，今天想起來也真是不可思議。

In the 60s, people were not familiar with real estate. I did not understand the process since I came from a farming village. It was a miracle that I could overcome all obstacles and successfully made money. I could run high-tech business while I did not know anything about alternating current and direct current at the beginning. In addition, my business was quite success and I had the record of the best seller in Taiwan. It was really unbelievable.

　　我不懂貿易，自己上網，找到我要的產品，只透過電話跟國外洽談之後，就這樣進口銷售，每年都有不錯的利潤，對我來說賺錢好像很容易。

I did not understand trading so I search for products online, and communicate with companies overseas on the phone. I imported some products and made good profit every year. To me, making money seems easy.

人生事事難預測。我的一生當中發生很多預料不到之事，回想以前的遭遇，再與現在的生活比較，都會懷疑自己是否正在做夢。想起父親騎著腳踏車載我到火車站的情景，當時我是個懵懂的小孩，獨自一個人遠離家鄉，又舉目無親，這種情況之下，實在難以想像自己會有今天的一點成就。

Life is unpredictable. There were many unpredictable things in my life. Thinking of my past and compared them to my current life, I often wonder if I was dreaming. I remembered the time when Father rode me to the station on his bicycle. I was just a kid knowing nothing but gone away from home. It was really hard to imagine that I would have the successful achievement today under the situation back then.

在我剛開始要演出我精彩的人生時，就差點被病魔打倒。名醫判了我死刑，躺在急診室面臨死亡的那一刻，心裡還想著，自己一定沒有機會活著回家。這種經歷很少人有機會體驗到，而我遇到了，所幸最後又能夠恢復健康。

I was knocked down by illness when I was just about to perform my colorful life. The doctor told me there was little hope while I lied in the bed of the emergency room. I thought I had no chance of going home. Seldom people have this kind of experience, but I did. Thus I felt grateful that I could recover.

當初我來到台北，連寫信回家也不會，信寄出後又被退回，而今天我竟有能力耐著性子完成這一本書，這些事情在我還沒一一實現之前，我從沒想過自己能做得到。所以說：人生的命運還是要由自己去掌握、運轉。

When I first came to Taipei, I could not even write a letter. The letter had been sent out and back, but I could have the patience to write this book now. Before accomplishing these things, I never thought that I could do this. Therefore, we have to hold on to our own fate, and control it.

雖然事業有成，一生中使我感到最安慰的不是賺了很多錢或有兒女、子孫，而是聽聞佛法。學佛可以了生脫死，不再六道輪迴，往生西方極樂世界。今生有機會當人，是宿世修得，所以要珍惜今生，要趁這難得機緣，求往西方極樂世界，才是今生無上重要大業。生在人間，很多事或物都可以用金錢解決了事，可是求永遠活在人間不死，或往生西方極樂世界，這二件事，花再多的金錢也無法辦到，必需依靠自己有堅定的信心。如果信心猶如「鋼」那麼堅定，不花一毛錢，也可達到目的地—西方極樂世界。生命的意義不只要創造自己，還需要利益他人。

Although my business went well, I made a lot of money and had children and grandchildren, they were not what soothe me most in my life. Knowing and understanding of Buddhism is the greatest thing in my life. Understanding Buddhism could know more about life, accept life, and fear not about death. I did not spin in the six great division of the karma wheel and could die in a pure land. I could be a human in the present life is because I planted a good cause in the previous life, so I need to treasure my life. I need to use the special opportunity to pray for living in a pure land after life. That is the most important thing in life. Since we are mortal, many things could be solved by money. However, wishing to be immortal or living in a pure land after life could not be done no matter how much money you spent. You have to be confident and had a firm decision. If you are as confident and determined as steel, you could reach the goal- living in a pure land after life not spending a dollar. The meaning of life is to not only create ourselves, but also benefit others.

「若言下相應，即共論命運；若實不相應，合掌令歡喜。」
"If the words are appropriate then we revealed the meanings of fate; if it is not appropriated words then we rejoice together in prayer"

最後願望

The last hope

　　有了生命才會有死亡，每個人都非常害怕死亡，因為不知死亡後會往何處去？這當然心裡會很恐懼。如果人在死亡之前能夠選擇自己想要去的地方，對死亡就不會有絲毫的害怕，並且會感到很快樂、平靜、安詳，這種心境猶如要出國去旅行的心情。要建立一個死亡無懼的心態，這也是人生最重要的事。

　　We live, and we die. People are afraid of death because we do not know where we will go after death. This would frighten us. If we could choose the place where we wanted to go before death, we would not be afraid of death. Instead, we would feel happy, peaceful, and quiet. The state of mind is like going on a trip. Establishing a fear-free feeling towards death is one of the most important things in life as well.

　　我們都了解遲早要面對死亡，可是我們總認為那是未來、是很久以後的事，我不必去想它。其實人的壽命是不一定的，死亡無理、無序可循。任何人、任何時候都有可能會死，不論老幼、貧富、生病或健康。講到死亡，大家都很惶恐，可是沒有理所當然的事，強壯健康的人不知所以，突然說走就走；而體弱多病的人則反而拖很久的時間。每個人都很照顧自己這個身體，也相信它可以使用很久，但事實卻經常與希望相違背。人的身體可說是脆弱、不堪一擊的，身體是靠飲食來維持生命健康，可是食物也會讓人生病而導致死亡。沒有任何東西或方法能夠保證長命百歲，因此心裡要隨時準備往生的心態，當無常來臨時，才不會恐懼。

　　We knew we would have to face death sooner or later, but we think that is in the long future so we do not need to think about it. Actually we do not know how long we live. Death is unpredictable and everywhere among us. Anyone would die in any minute no matter how old you are, whether you are rich or poor, and no matter you were healthy or not. People get panic when it comes to death, but things were just uncertain. A strong and healthy person could die in a sudden, and the person suffer in illness might live long. People take good care of their body health but often things went the way it should not be. Our human body is actually weak and easy-defeat. We depended on food to maintain healthy, but food could make us sick or even kill us. Nothing could make us immortal. Thus we have to prepare ourselves to the variable life so as not to be afraid.

生命走到了這個階段，我雖然已經感到非常滿足，但我還是熱切的想要追求更豐富的生命，所以我將利用我的餘生精進佛法。佛教徒瞭解「無常」，做人真辛苦。為了自己、親情、利益、慾望，擔心未來的種種事情，有種種的妄想生起來，心無法清淨，煩惱一大堆，痛苦就隨著而來。佛教是教人不執著、放下、無所求、少欲無為，就不會被慾望束縛，就會活得自在。學佛最終目標是要離苦得樂，脫離人間八苦：生、老、病、死、愛別離、怨憎會、求不得、五陰熾盛，了生脫死，不再六道輪迴，求往西方極樂世界。

Though I am very satisfied with my life in this stage, I am still passionate in pursuing a more meaningful life. Thus, I use my spare time to study Buddhism. Buddhists understand the phrase "uncertainty". It is so hard to be human. We have to worry about ourselves, relatives and friends, benefit, desire, and future. All the concerns could not make our heart peace. Pain comes with worrying. Buddhism told people to be flexible, to let go easily, and to desire less. We would be care free not to be constraint by desire. The goal of studying Buddhism is to have joy instead of bitter, and to escape from the eight bitterness of life: birth, aging, sickness, death, leaving the ones we love, meeting the ones we hate, having nothing we want, and our body feeling pain. When we no longer stuck in the six great division of the karma wheel, we pray to live in the pure land.

在這本書裡，我說了很多做人的道理，對人要寬心、喜捨、忍辱、回饋社會、幫助真正需要幫助的人等等。這些我都還沒做得很好，因此要更加精進，才能夠讓自己滿意。所以我常提醒自己要加油。希望更多的人也能試著去感恩、分享、回饋，讓我們有一個更美好的世界。

I had talked a lot about life in this book: treating others nicely and kind, willing to part or let go, enduring contempt, giving feedback to the society, helping those who were in need···etc. I did not do these things well so I need to improve to satisfied myself. I often remind myself to be better, and hoping that others could as well trying to be thankful, willing to share, and giving feedback. Let's have a better world together.

有一天，如果我的肉體使用期限到了，往生幾天後，不必擇日火化，更不需要設置靈堂或告別儀式，我剎那間就到極樂世界了。如有親友不捨我往生而悲傷、哭泣，這些動作是多餘又可笑的，大家的費心是為何事呢？（本來無一物，何處惹塵埃）請大家要準備自己往生的偉業大事吧。把臭皮囊火化後的骨灰，放在任何一個地方都可以（樹葬、海葬皆歡喜）。之後也不需要子孫膜拜或紀念，那只是一罈灰塵。枉費精神和時間去做這種無聊之事，還不如利用這些時間，可以多接觸佛法或做一些對人間更有意義之事。利用時間和金錢，幫助真正需要幫助的人，這才是真正孝敬父母。

If one day my day has come, I do not need to be cremated after I died. I also do not need a funeral or a funeral hall. I would be in the pure land at the moment. It would be too much or ridiculous if relatives and friends mourned for me. Why concern? (While there is nothing, why falls the dust?) Please prepare for your own death. I am fine with wherever my ashes put (either under some trees, or in the ocean are fine). I do not want my grandchildren to remember me, because that is just an ash bottle. It would be more meaningful to study Buddhism or do some meaningful things in life rather than wasting time on such thing. Using time and money on those who really needed help is truly showing respect to our parents.

　　希望我的子孫不會像我小時候農村老人家說的：「在生不孝，死了拜豬頭」。如果父母還活著的時候，不孝順他們，死後才準備豐富的祭品祭拜，這是一種對父母的侮辱，令人髮指。我寫了二首偈語，當作生命最後目標：
　　明往西方心自在，
　　道生極樂笑顏開；
　　往日學佛脫苦海，
　　生在淨土皈如來。

　　觀音慈悲渡眾生，
　　勢至菩薩現在前；
　　阿彌陀佛來接引，
　　誓願同生極樂界。

　　I hope that my grandchildren would not be like the elders said when I was little, "Showing no respect to elders now, praying with a feast to respect after they died." It is an insult to our parents not showing respect to them when they are still around, but preparing a big feast to remember them after they had gone.
　　I wrote two Buddhist's chants to be my last goal of life:
　　I feel free going to Heaven,
　　I feel happy of my life.
　　I study Buddhism for joy,
　　I follow my goals to a pure land.

　　Pray for us all the Mercy God
　　Great God shows up now
　　The Buddha comes to lead
　　Swear to live in the harmony

讀後心得

Book reviews

台灣世界展望會小朋友讀後心得 -- 筱薇

Book review from the children of World Vision Taiwan , Shiao Wei

Dear 陳伯伯：

　　看了陳伯伯的書之後，我發覺了一件事，人的「命運」不是自己能掌控的，但「運命」卻可以靠自己扭轉，這在之前的我，根本不會去想這些問題，但看了陳伯伯的書，才開始思考這些問題的。

Dear Mr. Chen, I realized one thing after reading your book. We do not control our own fate, but we could change our fortune. I started to think about this after I read your book.

　　同時也對於陳伯伯走過的人生歷程感到了不可思議，十四歲吔！十四歲就獨自一人上台北，還真是太令人震驚了，十四歲我們都還在懵懵懂懂、溫室裡的花朵，根本不了解外面的風風雨雨，甚至有些人二十四歲了，找不到工作，在家當「啃老族」。

Meanwhile, I was surprised by the life experiences Mr. Chen had. Fourteen! It was unbelievable to go to Taipei alone at the age of fourteen. We were ignorant kids like flowers in the green house at fourteen not knowing what has happened out there. Some people even did not have a job at the age of twenty-four, and live on their parents.

　　或許陳伯伯上學的時間還比我們短，但他卻比任何人都還成功，這應證了一句話：三分天注定、七分靠打拚。也讓我們了解，命運雖然不能扭轉，但可以在這些考驗裡面學習到更多的東西，從失敗中求取成功嘛！

Perhaps Mr. Chen spent lesser time in school than we did, but he is more successful than any of us. This proofs that "Thirty percent predestined, seventy percent earned". I also understand that though we could not change our fate, we could learn more in the experiences and be success out of failure.

還有一句話也讓我印象深刻，人會有一個貴人，醫生明明就說沒救了，但卻遇到了貴人，使自己好了起來，這可能就是陳伯伯上輩子修的福報吧！或許我們真多該學學陳伯伯，多做善事，替自己多積點陰德。

One thing that impressed me most is we would have a lucky charm in our life. The doctor announced the death with a hopeless voice, but a lucky charm saved Mr. Chen. This is the good cause from Mr. Chen's previous life. We should learn from Mr. Chen, doing kind things and give ourselves more good cause.

真的非常感謝您，因為最近有發生了一些事情，使我信心備受打擊，甚至更沒有活下去的希望，是看了您的書，我才覺得陳伯伯可以，我也可以，或許是這樣，我才有勇氣面對接下來的挑戰，而我終於熬過了，所以真的非常感謝您，帶給我們這本好書，讓我能夠啟發和受到感動。

I really appreciate you. I had some difficulties recently that I felt depressed. But after reading your book, I thought if you could do it, why couldn't I. Maybe that's what keeps me going. I overcame difficulties and have the courage to face the coming challenge. Thank you very much for this good book which inspired me and touched me.

祝
　　身體健康
Wish you all the best.

「浮雲遊子求前程，勇於表現萬事成。」
"A traveler like floating cloud pursues their own goal; it
could be succeed that they behave himself well"

國家圖書館出版品預行編目資料

命運・運命 —— 一個鄉下孩子的台北夢(中英對照) / 陳明道
岳彤、李婷莉、余坤興、陳立峰 譯
　--初版--
臺北市：博客思出版事業網：2014.7
ISBN：978-986-5789-25-1(平裝)
783.3886

103012114

1.陳明道　2.臺灣傳記

台灣人物奮鬥系列　2

命運・運命 —— 一個鄉下孩子的台北夢 (中英對照)

作　　者：陳明道
譯　　者：岳彤、李婷莉、余坤興、陳立峰
美　　編：謝杰融
封面設計：謝杰融
執行編輯：張加君
出 版 者：博客思出版事業網
發　　行：博客思出版事業網
地　　址：台北市中正區重慶南路1段121號8樓14
電　　話：(02)2331-1675或(02)2331-1691
傳　　真：(02)2382-6225
E—MAIL：books5w@gmail.com
網路書店：http://bookstv.com.tw/
　　　　　http://store.pchome.com.tw/yesbooks/
　　　　　博客來網路書店、博客思網路書店、華文網路書店、三民書局
總 經 銷：成信文化事業股份有限公司
劃撥戶名：蘭臺出版社 帳號：18995335
香港代理：香港聯合零售有限公司
地　　址：香港新界大蒲汀麗路36號中華商務印刷大樓
　　　　　C&C Building, 36,Ting, Lai, Road, Tai,Po, New,Territories
電　　話：(852)2150-2100　傳真：(852)2356-0735
總 經 銷：廈門外圖集團有限公司
地　　址：廈門市湖裡區悅華路8號4樓
電　　話：86-592-2230177
傳　　真：86-592-5365089
出版日期：2014年7月 初版
定　　價：新臺幣 280 元整（平裝）
ISBN：978-986-5789-25-1(平裝)

版權所有・翻印必究